The Golden Thread

The Golden Thread

by

Nettie Vander Schrier

MOODY PRESS
CHICAGO

Library of Congress Cataloging in Publication Data

Vander Schrier, Nettie.
    The golden thread.
    1. Vander Schrier, Nettie.   2. World War, 1939-1945
—Personal narratives, Dutch.   3. Netherlands—History
—German occupation, 1940-1945.   4. World War, 1939-
1945—Netherlands.   5. Salvationists—Netherlands—
Biography.   I. Title.
D811.5.V36   1982   940.54′82′492   82-14497
ISBN 0-8024-0173-2

    2 3 4 5 6 Printing/LC/Year 87 86 85 84 83

Printed in the United States of America

To my Jake

Contents

Foreword

Nettie Vander Schrier is a woman of great faith! She is also a woman of action. *The Golden Thread* presents a dramatic account of how God graciously leads, lovingly cares, and sovereignly provides for His own people in all situations.

We all live in unredeemed bodies in the midst of an unredeemed creation. We have a host of enemies that constantly oppress us. But we are not alone! Men of all ages faced these same complexities of life and won the battle. The good news for every believer is that God is able to use even the hard times in our lives to make us better people, and that He will give us grace to be triumphant in all kinds of hardships.

As you read *The Golden Thread,* Hebrews 11:6 should come alive for you: "And without faith it is impossible to please Him, for he who comes to God must believe that He is, and that He is a rewarder of those who seek Him."

My prayer is that God will use this book to be a blessing to all who read it and bring encouragement and hope and victory to every believer. May God's Spirit move upon your spirit as you see His powerful provision in *The Golden Thread.*

> Dr. John F. Thielenhaus
> Senior Pastor
> Parma Heights Baptist Church,
> Cleveland, Ohio

Preface

"There is no limit to what God will do with a soul completely dedicated and sold out to Him."

Our young minister asked those attending the service that Sunday morning to respond to the challenge of selling-out to the Lord. When no one signified willingness to do so by raising a hand, perhaps he felt it a wasted sermon. But oh, how God worked in my heart during the week that followed! In the quietness of my kitchen, I began to think about the words spoken in that sermon. I realized that for much too long I had been on the sidelines, not doing my part for the Lord. The responsibility of bringing up five children and seeing to the needs of my husband had taken up most of my time.

With tears in my eyes I prayed, "Lord, I love You with all my heart. I love also Your Word. What You can do with a fifty-five-year-old woman is beyond me, but all I have or am or will be is in Your hands. Use me and make my inner ear sensitive to Your calling."

How remarkably God changed my life upon my "selling out" to Him. I found new joy in living and a deep longing to study my Bible. Prayer became a joyful experience, a real union between my Lord and me. With the joy came a longing to please Him in my daily life.

Not too long after this change took place, I was in a small country church that was having evangelistic services. The old and gray evangelist stood in front of a wooden easel and drew the story of Jesus with chalk while music played in the background. I was fascinated! I learned later that this man had traveled for forty years, spreading the gospel by drawing his sermons. Right then and there I knew that this was how I could serve, though in a slightly different way.

During the years when my children were small, I used to grasp time for myself when they were busy or asleep. In those moments, I would paint pictures in oil. People who saw my paintings around my little home would remark about my talent. I was always quick to answer that I didn't see what good it was doing me. Of course, even then God had a plan for my life all worked out.

That winter I traveled many miles to a nearby city where the dear old evangelist patiently taught me to tell a story, quickly drawing pictures to the accompaniment of music, so I might spread the gospel of God's redeeming love. When I felt ready to draw my first picture, my loving husband, who can make anything with his hands, made my first wooden easel. It soon proved too small for large audiences, so he made me a beautiful folding easel of chrome pipe, with a fluorescent black light and five colored bulbs.

I gave my first performance in our church library for a dozen Sunday school kids. I felt very shaky, but all went well. After another Sunday school class, the big day arrived when I was privileged to draw in front of my own church congregation. I was accompanied by two lovely friends, one singing a solo, the other playing the piano. These two women went with me that first year from place to place until I was forced to tape my background music because of the many requests I received. I give all honor to God for souls won through the use of a little piece of chalk.

One day the choir director at my church asked me to give my testimony during the Easter service. In gathering my thoughts together, I was suddenly aware of a golden thread that had been spun throughout my life thus far. From that day on, I included my testimony with my drawings.

When people began to ask if I had ever thought of writing a book, I laughed, but slowly the idea became an urgency within me. As the words began to flow, I prayed that God would help me to share with others how marvelously He has brought me through the fires of hell into a radiantly beautiful life of walking with Him.

Acknowledgments

The golden thread is still being woven. By much prayer, the right people were sent by "the Master Weaver" at just the right moments. Their loving efforts made it possible for me to write this book.

Mrs. Paul (Esther) Baxendale and Mrs. Augustus (Bobbi) Carlino worked tirelessly in the strong belief that this story should be published. For hours and weeks and months Esther transformed my Dutch-English sentences, and Bobbi typed the first draft.

At a time when it seemed that the weaving would be delayed, God provided a couple from Oberlin, Ohio, to continue the work—Norma and Hans-Axel Stechow. Norma took over the endless typing, and Hans helped greatly with the editing. They believed that the story would be published and encouraged me to see it through.

The understanding of my husband, Jake, and Paul, the youngest of our five children, was invaluable. Night after night, they endured hot dogs and hamburgers and considered them a full course dinner when french fries were added. Their love sustained me.

Throughout the creation of *The Golden Thread,* God's hand has been clearly evident, touching all who have spent so much time, and creating in them an enthusiasm for our "project." To Him their gifts and mine are offered in glory.

1

Father's Reassurance

"Oh, Daddy, Daddy, why does Mother hate me so?"

Swinging the door wide open from my father's workshop, I ran sobbing straight into his arms, away from the shrill screaming voice of my mother. Even within the safety of his enclosing arms, I still could hear the echo of her voice.

"Get her away, get her away from me!"

In my haste to get out, I had lost one of my slippers, but I didn't notice. Though bewildered, I felt safe with Dad. While he ran a hand through my long blonde hair and wiped my tears with a big red handkerchief, he calmly said, "It is all right, little one, it is all right. Tell me just what happened." Between sobs, I told Dad all about what had happened that morning.

"I helped Mother dry the dishes. Then we made the beds. After that Mother said she was going to mend the socks and I could color in that big coloring book you gave me at Christmas. So I colored a picture just for her."

"What was in the picture, Nettie?"

"Oh, it was a pretty picture. There were three children in it. I gave one little girl a red dress and the boy a blue suit, and I made yellow long hair on the one girl and yellow hair on the other girl. I made her four years old just like me. My hair is yellow, isn't it, Daddy?"

"Yes, it is, Nettie."

"And Daddy, I gave the boy dark hair. Boys have dark hair, don't they, Daddy?"

"Yes, honey, they have dark hair."

"And after that then I drew a pussycat. The picture was so pretty. I thought she would like it. And so I walked up behind her and said, 'Here, Mother, for you.' She looked at it—and then she started screaming. And more screaming that I should get away from her. 'Get away from me! Get her away from me!' "

Again I sobbed and sobbed. "Daddy, I hate her too."

"Hush! Hush!" Daddy said.

When I tried to say more he said, "Stop it, little one; your mother cannot help it!" More or less to himself he said, "I should have known it this morning—she spoke hardly a word, and she looked so pale." Then his words were directed at me again.

"I am sorry, honey, I could have prevented all this, but I did not know she had one of her days. Your mother is sick," he said while he stroked my hair.

"Does she have a tummyache?"

"No, honey, she is sick with a broken heart." Slowly Dad began telling me in his soft, soothing voice a story I vaguely remembered in part.

"First of all, get it good in your mind that your mother does *not* hate you." And wiping my tears again, he told me as tenderly as only he could why Mother seemed so angry.

"Your mother does not hate you, but sometimes when she sees you, she is reminded that there were once three of you. She thinks of Maria, with the long blonde hair and eyes as blue as a summer sky.

14

And of Frankie, your twin brother—the son your mother always wanted. We were the happiest family you could imagine." Dad's face became so sad, and his eyes were wet. He sat there drying my eyes and rubbing his own.

"Daddy, don't cry, please don't cry. I won't cry if you won't."

"All right, honey," he agreed. "Your mother made a beautiful white lace dress entirely by hand for Maria, remember? And then we went to the big city to buy you and Frankie navy blue sailor suits—both alike—with big collars and white stripes. We took the three of you to the photographer and had your pictures taken, because we were so proud of you. We visited the big church where the benches had doors on the side and where you kids had to stand up in order to see the choir members enter. One of them was your mother, and we would wait until she had given us a faint smile before she sat down. And the minister would come dressed in a long black robe too. Before he would climb up to the *preekstoel* he would stand still for a moment to pray. And then the big organ would play, and when the singing or preaching was too long, Maria would try to count all the lights in the huge chandelier. All three of you were baptized there.

"Then on Sunday after dinner we would sit in the parlor while mother played the organ and we all sang the old hymns. Nettie, can you remember still when Mother played the organ?"

"Yes, Daddy, I remember a little, but that was when I was very small. Oh, Daddy, I wish she would play a song for me!"

"We were such a happy family, never thinking for a minute that things would change so soon. That following January, the ugly sickness entered our

15

home. Maria was the first to get sick. Old Doctor Bruin was called to the house. He said it was only the flu, and Mother and I believed him. But two days later, Maria died in your mother's arms. The same day, you and Frankie got violently ill with the same sickness. An ambulance came and took both of you to the big hospital in Rotterdam. There Frankie died exactly a week after Maria. She had been buried in her white lace dress, and Frankie was buried in his sailor suit. You had your third birthday in the hospital that same month. The nurses fastened a flag on each corner of your bed because we both—Mother and Dad—were so happy we still had you." He hugged me tenderly.

"That was almost two years ago, and Mother has never been the same. She would not bring her sorrow to the Lord Jesus. Her flashes of anger were not only directed at you and me, but also at God. She refused to go to church and would not speak to our dear old preacher. She quit the choir, and the locked organ and the music books gathered dust."

I began sobbing. "Dad, are Maria and Frankie in heaven now?"

"Yes, they are, Nettie. They are both in heaven by Jesus."

"But I'm alone here, Dad."

After a moment of silence he said with a little tone of excitement, "I have a surprise for you. Next month when the pear tree is blooming and summer is almost here, you will get a new sister or brother. Maybe that will change things around here!"

I jumped off Daddy's lap and looked at him with my eyes as big as apples. "We are going to have a real live baby in this house?" Dad nodded his head. I jumped up and down; I could hardly contain all that joy. Dancing on my tiptoes, I screamed, "Oh, goody, goody!" And with hundreds of questions, I blurted, "What will it be, a brother or a sister? What will we name it? And, and, and—"

"Stop, stop, little one," my father laughed. His face was full of happy wrinkles. I threw both of my arms around his neck and hugged him over and over and said, "Oh, Daddy, I love you so."

"That's my girl," he said. "Let's be good to Mother in this last month."

"But Daddy, where does the baby come from? Does God send it?"

"Yes, Nettie, God has a lot to do with it, because He is making that baby. That baby is growing close to Mother's heart. That close." He held his thumb and forefinger about an inch apart.

"Did I grow near Mother's heart?"

"Yes, Nettie, you, too."

"And Frankie, too?"

"Yes, Frankie, too. Both of you side by side."

"Okay, let's go and tell Mother."

"Now, wait a minute, little one. This is a secret between you and me. We're not going to breathe a word to Mother. She's sick, remember? We've got to take real good care of her, and I know you'll help because you're a big girl. You're four years old, after all. Now, let's go. Where's your slipper? You have only one! Your sock is wet! You must have left it in the house. Well, I'll have to carry you—hold on." Up came Daddy's big arms, and he lifted me like a sack of feathers. He walked laughing through the yard and up to the kitchen door, opened it up, and set me on the floor. And there was Mother.

I felt uneasy, but it was all right. She did not look at me. Dad went to her because she was stirring something on the top of the stove. "How are you doing?" he asked her.

She answered, "I think I'm OK."

Dad said, "Well, I am hungry, aren't you, little one? Let's set the table for Mother."

That night I could not sleep for excitement. A real baby in our house? What would it be? A brother or a sister? What should we name it? When I finally fell asleep, I dreamed about all the wonderful things about to happen.

Finally it was just as Dad told me—one day as the pear tree was blooming my new baby sister arrived. At first she slept most of the time. Her fingers and toes were so tiny. She brought smiles to all of us. We were all very happy with the little bundle called "Nellie."

nettie 1982.

2

The House on the Lake

Our little brick house, heavy with a clinging blanket of ivy, sagged a little to the left with an impression of tiredness. Before Dad, Mother, and I lived there, it sheltered our grandparents and their families. The stone steps leading to the front door had turned moss-green with age. The feet of many visitors over the years had worn indentations in the stone. On the solid walnut door, the mail slot and heavy copper knocker were polished as though they were gold. The fresh white curtains in the clean shiny windows gave the house a warm welcoming glow. Beneath the front steps a casement window let light into the cellar, where all the crocks of vegetables stood. Green beans, sauerkraut, endives, and others were covered with a salty brine to keep them from spoiling. The row of pots waiting to be used in the wintertime was covered with red and white checkered cloths.

If you walked farther along the side of our home, you could go through a white trellis gate. Our visitors were always delightfully surprised at the abundance and variety of flowers in every color of the rainbow. At the base of an apple tree was an old wooden bench with tubs spilling over with bright red geraniums on each side of it. Just before the frost hit, Dad brought those geraniums into the basement to hang there all winter. They looked like old dead branches, but in the spring, when he was through nursing them, they again became full, blooming plants. The Netherlands' rich soil and frequent rains contributed greatly to the always luscious flowers.

Behind our garden stood Dad's workshop, all by itself. An oil heater made the place cozy and warm in winter and just right on crisp mornings. I had a place all my own on a high stool next to the bench where Dad did his work. He was an interior decorator. Often he would bring in priceless heirlooms for repair by his able hands. Shelves held cans of paints and varnishes and all the books of drapery and wallpaper samples. In the spring new books would arrive, and I was given the discarded ones to be cut and pasted to my heart's desire.

On the wall between the door and the four-paned window hung Dad's fishing gear with his cap and raincoat. He was an expert fisherman. He could just walk out the door of his workplace to find his rowboat bobbing up and down on the lake behind our house. I was not allowed in the boat, because Mother feared I would fall out. That lake was beautiful, not only the pride of our family but of thousands of people who would come on weekends to enjoy it.

We lived on the outskirts of Rotterdam, a world harbor city. Big ocean liners from all over the world stopped to refuel and to bring in tourists. In the summer, people would come from the city and knock on our door to ask for the key to the big iron gate, for Father was the caretaker of the wharf where their sailboats lay at anchor. If the weekend promised good weather, Mother, Dad, and I would sit watching the sails go up and the boats then picking up speed in the wind.

On Saturday, the newspaper would announce the coming of a sailboat race, always held on Sunday afternoon so that church services were uninterrupted. Afterward hundreds of people would walk with their families in Sunday attire to the west side of the lake. It was like a grand Easter parade. On that side of the lake were green fields where children could run and play, and there were benches for others to sit and watch the races. You could see mothers pushing carriages, showing off their babies as they strolled along. The fathers and sons would debate about the racers and their boats, while young folks would walk hand in hand by the beautiful lake. It was a festive way to spend a Sunday afternoon.

On the south side of the lake stood two windmills called "the twins." On weekdays you could see their big arms turning round and round. One mill ground wheat and rye. Right there you could buy the flour in a sack bearing a picture of the mill and the miller. On Sundays, when the mill was not in operation, that enterprising miller would place small iron ta-

21

bles and chairs outside his mill and sell tea and lemonade.

The other mill was our favorite, though. When the wind was from the south, our house, our garden,

The cinnamon mill.   nettie '82

and everything in the neighborhood smelled of cinnamon that the mill was grinding for shipment to markets around the world.

In the winter, the scene along the lake took on a different beauty. As soon as the ice was officially tested for strength and safety, the newspaper would announce the opening of the skating season. Dutch children would already have been skating on the canals back and forth to school. But now the great moment had arrived; the lake was safe for the skaters who came from all over. Early in the morning a city crew would arrive with shovels and huge brooms to clean wide paths over the ice. This enabled the skaters to reach the two little islands in the middle of the lake and also to skate past the two picturesque turning windmills. Ice vendors would sell hot chocolate from their carts as well as a special hard candy known as *polka brokken*. This hot, spicy confection was sold only at that time of year. As soon as we could smell the cinnamon from the mill across the lake, we knew that the thaw would end our winter fun and spring would soon arrive.

3

Spring Is on the Way

It seemed winter would never come. The fall weather, with its storms and rains, almost had us convinced that it would be a mild winter. But with the coming of January, winter was in its full glory. Long icicles were hanging from the corner of our house. The roof, bushes, and sidewalks all were white. Even the old-fashioned lantern by the front door was wearing a high white hat of freshly fallen snow.

Earlier in the day, Dad had come out and said, "Nettie, let's make an enormous snowman." It was so huge that my father had to climb a ladder to plant his fishing cap on top of the snowman's head. The snowman had a carrot nose and a broom where its hands should have been. Mother, with Nellie on her arm, had been quietly watching us through the kitchen window. She motioned me to come to the door and handed me Grandpa's pipe to place in its mouth. We all thought it was the best snowman ever built.

"Let's go inside to warm ourselves," said Dad. "Mother will make us all some hot tea." Revived by the delicious, warming tea, we hurried back outside. This time Dad took me along to chop a hole in the ice to measure its thickness. "Tonight (or at least to-morrow, on your birthday) the lake's sure to be declared safe for skating. The official start of the ice-skating season will be reported in the newspaper. It will be a big day for you, so you'd better get some sleep."

Tired to the bone, I lay in bed. Mother had said that the earlier I went to bed, the faster my birthday would arrive. My bed was so cozy and warm. Every night my mother would fill a small stone bottle with hot water and cover it with one of Dad's old socks. The sock kept my feet from burning, and the stone bottle assured me of a warm bed to crawl into. I could hardly wait to find out what my birthday present could be. I would have to search for it as always. I started thinking of all the places it could be hidden, and soon fell fast asleep.

I awoke with a jolt, thinking that it must be early. I lay in bed listening for the familiar early morning sounds. Outside it was already getting light, or so I thought. I was sure I would soon hear the bedroom door squeak and Father tiptoe to the kitchen stove to rake the ashes out. Then he would open the outside door, slip into his wooden shoes, and spread the ashes on the snowy path as he walked.

In my imagination I could even "hear" him open the door of the workplace and with a loud bang, shut it behind him. Even with my eyes closed, I could follow his morning routine step by step. I accompanied him many a morning when it was not as cold as it was today. First he would light the kerosene lamp and then the oil stove; later on, when he was ready for work, his place would be warm and cozy. Next he would fill the wicker basket with old papers and kindling, which were neatly stacked in the corner. He loaded his arms with logs as he left; the workplace door slammed again. This noise alerted the neighbor's dog and the birds. With the dog barking and the birds singing, Dad would come into the kitchen and start the fire. Pretty soon the water kettle would start making funny noises. Then Mother would begin preparing breakfast.

But no such thing *this* morning! I could see light coming through the closed curtains. Dad must have overslept. I shivered as I crawled out of bed and put on my slippers. As I went to my parent's bedroom, I was careful not to awaken Nellie, my little sister. For sure, she would start crying and get me into trouble. I went to Dad's side of the bed. Instantly he woke up. "What's the matter, little one?" he whispered.

"Wake up, Dad; you overslept. It is already light, and it is my birthday today! I am six today, remember?"

Our talking woke Mother, and Nellie began to cry! I began to feel that something wasn't just right. I said louder than I intended to, "Doesn't anybody remember it's my birthday?"

By now Dad had found his glasses and was staring at the alarm clock. He began laughing. I was so glad to hear him laugh, even though I did not understand.

"Look here, little one, it's only midnight. The light is from the full moon."

He lifted me up as he pulled the curtains open far enough that I could see the big round shiny moon. So he put me to bed again and said, "Close those pretty eyes of yours and before you know it, it will be morning. Good night!" He kissed me and left.

When I finally woke up that morning, I wanted to be sure that it was day now, so I opened the curtains and took a peek outside. A coat of freshly fallen snow covered everything. The trees and bushes glittered; snow and ice clung to every branch. The clothespins on the washline looked like little white birds waiting for food. The lake looked like a gigantic cake covered with powdered sugar. I heard my parents in the kitchen. Excited and bubbling over, I dashed in. Immediately I saw that Mother was having one of her bad days. I was too young to realize that this birthday of mine reminded her of the loss of her two children. Instead of congratulating me on my sixth birthday, she left the room with tears in her eyes.

But Dad was prepared for this. He excitedly hugged and kissed me. "Happy birthday, dear Nettie!" I became impatient to find my present. Dad said, "Look on the chair under the dish towel." I lifted the towel and saw the most beautiful iceskates a girl could ever wish for! The metal was so shiny that the blades looked like mirrors. The long shoelaces were as white as the snow.

My little sister Nellie, just sixteen months old, had crawled into the kitchen. Holding on to Daddy's lap, she was dancing up and down, sensing the joy around us. Her chubby little hands were reaching toward the skates. Her laughing and babbling even seemed to cheer Mother, who had returned to the kitchen. Now she wished me a happy birthday. I wanted so badly to be part of her love and I wanted to hug her for buying skates for me. But when I tried to hug her, she abruptly pulled away and gave me a disturbed look. I cringed, wondering what I had done wrong. What could have upset her so?

I heard Mother say, "Is it not about time to get dressed? Go to your father—*do* something—get out of here." I knew that she was still hurting when she looked at me. She lifted Nellie, hugging her, the child of her new beginning, and rejected the child of her painful past. A dislike for my mother was growing, or was it hate? It would take me many, many years to figure that out.

After breakfast I heard my father ask my mother, "Where did you put that old kitchen chair?" I wondered what he needed it for. "Go get your skates, Nettie."

When I returned, clutching my skates, he took my little hand in his large one, and off we went to his workplace. I was glad to be in our own cozy spot. I climbed onto my stool and watched. "Dad, what are you going to do?"

"Just wait," he said. "You'll see." Gripping the old kitchen chair with his big strong hands, he sawed off its back. I still wondered what he had in mind. Then he took a large board and fastened a handle to it.

"A shovel, you've made a shovel!" I cried.

Chuckling, he said, "Stay put until I've cleared some of the snow off the lake." It took a very long time for him to return; when he did, he looked like a snowman!

His glasses were all steamed up, and his nose was red. He stood slapping his arms around his waist to warm himself. Then he fastened my new skates over my high brown shoes. He had to wrap the ties around my ankles several times. I put on my warm winter coat, my mittens, and my hat. Over all that, a woolen scarf covered my head, nose, and ears. "You look like a mummy." He laughed. "Now you wait for me." Father opened a large drawer and got his skates out, too. Last winter he had covered the blades with grease so the metal would not rust. He now took a cloth and shined the iron blades. After knotting the strings, he hung the skates over his shoulder. "OK, let's go." He picked me up in his left arm and grabbed the mysterious stool with the sawed-off back and took off for the boat dock. When he put me down, he put the stool in front of me and said, "All right, Nettie, skate! Hold on to the stool—skate behind it as you push it over the slippery ice, and you will not fall and hurt yourself." But I could not even move one foot.

"How do I use my feet?" I was glad I was at least able to stand tall without falling.

"Wait a minute, I'll show you how." Dad took big long strokes to the left, then to the right. He looked so tall in his gray, hand-knitted sweater. The tassels on his cap went this way and that. He pushed the shovel in front of him at first to clear a long path; I

could see the blue-gray ice underneath. After he put his shovel down, he glided over the ice, his hands behind his back. The way he bent over with his head low made him look like a greyhound. That winter I learned to skate, and in my childish way, I felt like an expert.

Hand in hand, my father and I visited the little islands in the center of the lake. We had been looking at them from our kitchen window. They were too small for any houses; instead they were covered with bushes and trees. They were a mystery to me. We explored first one and then the other, but we found nothing except some glass jars that once belonged to some fishermen, maybe to hold their bait. But then I looked across and saw our old brick house covered with snow. "Look, Father! The house seems so small but so pretty from here; I can even see your workshed." Later we skated together to the other side of the lake near the two mills, so beautiful in their white mantles of snow.

One morning when we awakened, the smell of cinnamon from across the lake told us that the wind had shifted to the south. Soon the thaw would come, making way for Holland's tulips and daffodils. With some regret, I greased the blades of my skates and hung them on the rafters up in the attic of the little brick house on the lake. And with that, we said goodbye to a perfect winter.

4

Morning in the City

Tulip time had come to Holland. The fragrance of the hyacinths, the brightness of the daffodils, and the varied color of the tulips all made the countryside festive. Visitors from all over the world would soon come to see the many fields of flowers. Holland's cleanliness was its trademark, so just before the arrival of all those tourists, every housewife would clean her home and shine her windows. The narrow cobblestone sidewalks were scrubbed with soap and water. Everyone was in a holiday mood. In every Dutch home were bouquets of tulips, and bright geraniums decked the front windows.

In Holland, the new school year starts in March, so at this beautiful time of the year, I started school. It was a big event in the life of a little girl. Despite saying as little to me as possible, my mother made new clothes and knitted a sweater and heavy socks for me. Putting on my wooden shoes, and taking the lunch my mother prepared, I walked a mile and a half along the lake and then across a small picturesque bridge over the canal. At the top of that bridge I could see the big school in the distance.

Not only would I carry a sack lunch and my new school books, but I would have a little brown bag with two buttered slices of bread topped with sugar. Each day, halfway between home and school, I would pass a stable with a lonely donkey who had become a friendly face; so I started sharing my lunch with him. This beast was almost human. When he saw me coming, he would bray and bray, his eyes wide and his big teeth showing, until I laid down my books and my lunch to open *his* bag with the two slices of bread. What fun it was to watch him gobble them down. I hurried on, and I could hear him braying again—*hee-haw, hee-haw*—even until I crossed the little curved bridge over the canal.

I was very proud to learn to read and write, and I loved my teacher. In the afternoon, with my papers in my hand, I could hardly wait to tell my parents all the things I had learned that day.

My little sister Nellie was almost two years old when one day my Dad took me on his lap and said, "Nettie, we're going to have an addition to the family soon. Would you like a little brother this time?" I think he wanted a son, but it was not to be. Early in April, my sister Tine was born, making me (at six and a half) twice a big sister.

Pretty soon spring had passed to make way for one of Holland's wet summers. One didn't know from day to day what the weather would be. On one of the rare good days, I was in charge of watching Nellie and the baby in the backyard in the shade of the pear tree. Mother was taking in the wash. I was amused by Nellie, with her babblings and happy disposition. Dad was in his workplace, and Mother had just gone into the house with the wicker basket full of clean-smelling clothes. Unexpectedly a man in a police uniform came around to the backyard. "Are your mother and father home, little girl?" he asked. Before I could answer, my mother came hurrying around the house at the sound of the unfamiliar voice. She and the imposing figure in the uniform talked softly together. Then she called my dad, telling me to stay with the children. The three grown-ups went into the house and closed the door behind them. I was left outside with a hundred questions. It was all I could do to concentrate on my sisters, who could get into mischief at the blink of an eye.

Finally, the door opened again. The man in uniform shook hands with Father, who looked angry. Mother was beaming, and I was greatly puzzled. Dad went straight to his workplace, slamming the door behind him. I asked Mother, "Who was that man? Why did he come here?"

Mother explained. "He is a ranger from the park service. They have bought all the land along the north side. They're going to build a beautiful park with a sandy beach and a recreation area." Triumphantly she added, "We are going to move to the city, and I'm so glad. I hate this house. I hate it!"

Tears welled in my eyes. Moving? Where would we go? No workplace with a cozy heater, no boat bobbing on *our* lake, no skating anymore? Distraught, I ran to the workplace, where I found Dad bent over, his head in his hands. I sobbed and sobbed. Dad did not say a word, just patted my head. Suddenly he spoke: "Little one, it will be tough on you and me, but your mother will be happy. She has known lots of sorrow in this place, and she needs a change. You and I will find a way to be happy. Let's try to make *her* happy."

In looking back, it seems that it rained the rest of the summer. I said goodbye to all the familiar things, the lovely places so full of pleasantness and good times. When I heard that they would destroy the house to clear land for the recreation area, I was horrified. I would wake up screaming in the middle of the night. Dreams of the uniformed man cruelly tearing down our house and Dad's workplace kept running through my mind.

Finally on a bleak gray day, before the pears had fully ripened, the movers came. I went with my sisters to my aunt and uncle's home that day. When Dad came the following day to pick us up, we were caught up in the excitement of a small townhouse full of boxes. For the moment we forgot our disappointment, and played hide-and-go-seek.

Our new home was much more modern, but it had only a tiny yard. There would be no more fishing for minnows, no boat dancing on the lake. But Dad reassured me: "Nettie, you will soon find lots of friends your age to play with. It will be just as good for you here; you'll see."

The noise of the city was hard to bear at first. Everyone told us that in time we would not even hear it anymore. One thing that I *did* like though was going to school just around the corner. Schools in Holland are open from nine in the morning until noon and in the afternoon from two until four. I liked it better than the long walk to school and taking a lunch. The day seemed to go faster. Now I could spend so much more time playing with my many new friends.

I went to the Christian school there, not so much because I was a Christian, but because it was so nearby and convenient. The rules were intensely strict; Mother was strict, too. In a sense, school was a refuge. I learned so much from the Bible. I loved storytelling time—Joseph as a slave, Moses in the bullrushes, David and Goliath—their stories all became more and more familiar. I learned many a psalm by heart, as well as long passages from the Old and the New Testaments. Yet I had no idea how important these teachings and those of Jesus Christ our Savior and Lord would be to me in the years to come. At the time, I only knew God as someone who kept a record of all my bad and good deeds, and who would hold me responsible for every wrongdoing. I thought Him a disciplinarian, much like my teachers. His love toward us in sending His Son, Jesus Christ, to this earth was not clear to me then.

Years later I found out that most of the teachers were hired for this Christian school because they were members of our state church. Part of belonging to the *in* crowd was attending a respectable church. Almost everyone belonged, so anybody could be hired to teach if he or she had the academic requirements. This explained in part their cruelty to children whose parents were not socially acceptable or who belonged to the poorer class of society. The poorly dressed children were ridiculed for their too-big shoes or their outgrown dress, and they were never chosen for any privileges like being sent to carry messages to other classes. Though their treatment made me uneasy, I didn't have to worry about such discrimination, because my father was respected everywhere. I was well-dressed and not in need of anything.

Twice a week we would return to school in the evening for lessons in sewing, knitting, and weaving. But I was a child who could not sit still, and those awkward, long, slippery knitting needles caused me many a tear and brought me many correction slips for my parents to sign. My sewing wasn't much better. It was only through fear of my teachers' wrath that I tediously managed medium grades.

I had just started third grade when one day I was called to the principal's office and instructed to go to Mother's friend's house, where I also found Nellie and Tine. There I learned that while I was in school another sister had been born. Her name was Johanna. I was not thrilled at all. For me it meant more chores, more diapers to hang, more nights to awaken to the cry of a baby. When two years later *another* sister, Kobie, was born, I was so furious that I cried.

Dad took me aside and scolded me. "Nettie, get ahold of yourself! You should be delighted that God has brought you a healthy new sister. Just look at her tiny hands and her cute little toes! Remember, you were once just as small. I expect you to love your sisters and to act more grown up, for Mother needs your *help* much more than ever."

By that time, in the eyes of the world, Mother had completely recovered from her former sickness, but my father and I knew it was not so. Mother and I were never at ease with each other. It was clear to everyone that I was *Father's* daughter and that my sisters belonged to a different, newer era. To outsiders, we seemed to have all the things a happy family needed.

Father never got used to city life. He kept much more to himself. We had lived in that townhouse for only a year when Dad found one of Holland's familiar row houses for us near the lake. From the front window, we looked out over a canal and a lock. We could watch the motorboats being lifted up from the lowland canal to the height of the lake. The Dutch polders stretched as far as our eyes could see. A polder is a piece of land won by heaping on it the dredgings from the nearby lakes and letting it dry for several years until it could be used for planting grass or grain. This had been done for ages, and most of Holland had been won that way. There is a Dutch saying: "God made heaven and earth, but the Dutch made Holland."

We started attending a new church, and Mother took to attending the prayer meeting on Friday night. Dad would come home from work early so she could go. Even though she never said so, it seemed to fulfill some of her special needs. She went faithfully, every Friday.

In summer, Sunday afternoons became special times. Mother would take a nap with the littlest ones while Dad, Nellie, Tine, and I would go for a walk. We would head for the lake near the place where we used to live. I am sure Dad would have preferred wearing older clothes, but Mother would frown and insist that he go dressed up in his Sunday best. We girls would wear our frilly dresses. Before we left, all three of us would ask for a handkerchief, "A big one please!" Then off we would go. Aware of all the neighbors who also went for a Sunday stroll, Dad would tip his hat to the ladies and wave to the men. And you could hear them say with approval, "That's Jan with his children—so neat and well-behaved." If they had only known what we were up to.

The little ones would frolic ahead of us; they had learned the way. But I would stay with Dad. After all, I was already twelve and felt too mature to romp with my sisters. Besides, Dad and I would carry on quite a conversation. He would point out all the exciting things along the road, like a butterfly or an unusual tree or anything else that caught his fancy. When we talked, our walk to the old homesite did not seem so far. Soon we arrived at the place where our house used to stand. Dad never stopped there, but he *would* look painfully at the two little islands. Then he would hurry along as if to push away longing thoughts of the past.

We would go a little farther until we came to a place that few other people ever saw. It was halfway around the lake. There the road ended and became only a path. A little farther on, it branched off into our own private path. I believed that path was made solely by us, because we walked it dozens of times. We had to bow our heads to keep low branches from catching in our hair. Then we came to our own private meadow, surrounded by beautiful trees and overlooking "our" lake.

Out would come the handkerchiefs, spread on the grass. Then off would come Dad's hat with the small brim, and then his tie. He always folded his suit coat carefully and placed everything on the handkerchiefs. Rolling up his sleeves, he would play hide-and-seek with us. When we tired of that, we would look for lucky stones or four leaf clovers. All of a sudden Dad would say, "Let's hear how the worms are singing today," and out would come the other handkerchiefs. Carefully we would lay them out on the grass to avoid stains on the knees of our long white stockings. One by one we would kneel and put our ears to the grass to listen to the peculiar noises. Dad always told us the worms were singing. All too soon, he would look at his big pocketwatch and tell us that we should go back. We would look each other over to be sure we were presentable for the city world and head for home.

Sometimes the little ones would squeal on us and tell Mother. She would shake her head and say, "What would people say if they saw you kneeling with your ear on the ground to hear worms singing?" Looking first at me and then at Father, she would shake her head and say, "It takes one to understand one!"

But over Mother's shoulder, Dad would wink at me and I would wink back. It meant, "I understand you."

5

A Comfortable Life Ends

The year 1935 marked the first time that my vision extended beyond me and my family. In the big city of Rotterdam, new friends sometimes invited me to their homes.

For example, there was my friend Dini, whose father owned a small grocery store. When I arrived early for a visit with her and she was busy, I could often give a helping hand in the store. It was nice that they trusted me. I *tried* to come early, because working in the store fascinated me.

In addition to groceries, they also sold hot water from an enormous big tank. The women of the neighborhood could fill a small pail of three gallons for two cents, or a five-gallon one for three cents. On cleaning and laundry days, the women would cover the heavy, steaming pails with wooden boards and carry them home, sometimes up several flights of stairs. Their washing and scrubbing had to be done quickly before the water cooled.

Small bundles of wood, chopped and neatly stacked, were also sold at the store. Of course, any volunteer help was greatly appreciated. As pay, Dini's father usually gave us a huge jawbreaker candy.

Many a time when I packed the groceries, I would call to Dini's father, who would take a big book from under the counter. In it appeared long lists of names written in red. Many neighborhood families with jobless husbands owed large amounts of money. Mr. Jansen, Dini's father, was a good Christian man but far from dumb. He was well aware of who took advantage of his generosity and who was really in need. He would say to Vrouw Steen, a widow with three small boys, "Sure, take what you need; here, take some eggs along, too. You are too skinny." But to Vrouw Brand he would say, "Sorry, no bread! First bring me money." More and more people were without work, so the credit book came out for a very select few.

Then there was Corrie's family. Her father and big brother were laid off from the carpet factory for nearly a year. They fought constantly. "Why don't you forget that stupid factory job? Get yourself out and find something worthwhile!" Corrie's father thought his son, Lennard, was lazy. "The least you can do is get out of the house, instead of just lying around on your back. *Do* something with your life." Corrie and Lennard just kept picking at each other from sheer boredom. "You never help with the dishes." "Aw, that's woman's work." There was no money for the streetcar to go out for the day and no money for the smallest luxury.

I felt sorry for Lennard, though, for one day I met him on my way to pick up his sister. He looked so discouraged. "You know, Nettie, I am sick of this life," he said. "All day I knocked on doors for work. Some people did not even open the door. Others had a note posted on the front window—NO HELP WANTED. It drives me out of my mind. At home they yell at me for sleeping, but that makes the day go faster. What else can I do? A man must have a job to keep happy."

OUT OF WORK

"What are you willing to do?" I asked. "Is there a particular job you want?"

"No, Nettie, just so it's a job. As far as I know, I have been every place, but if there is even the smallest job open even for an hour or two, then they take a married man, and we teenagers are left out."

My other friend, "Beppie," and her sister Annie showed me another family situation different from my own. Together they had to do all the housework for their family of six. They also cared for the four smaller children. Her father was a shoemaker; his shop was in the basement of the apartment they lived in. Their mother was very sick with tuberculosis and had to be cared for in a sanitarium near the city of Wassenaar. Only her father could see her mother once a month. Although tuberculosis is now curable, it was then a very serious illness with no known cure.

There was much heartache all around. But the unemployment problem was the worst of all. It was beginning to affect every facet of the population. Banks were closed. Many street corners became gathering places for jobless, unhappy men. They were unable to provide for the most basic needs of their families. The mothers could not dress their children adequately and mended the already patched clothes.

There was no money for fresh fruit, vegetables, or milk, and that resulted in lowered resistance to sickness. There was so much illness everywhere: typhus, diphtheria, scarlet fever, and others. The future looked bleak for the poor. But there were still many middle-class families that fared pretty well. Every night the newspapers were full of stories about the lack of work and the ever slipping economy. They also talked about a new chancellor, Adolph Hitler, who ruled with an iron hand in Germany. Though he had once been imprisoned, he had now climbed to unheard of heights through shrewd political manipulation. He ruthlessly "annexed" surrounding countries like Austria and Czechoslovakia. He reigned by terror, calling himself the Führer of the Third Reich.

The jobless men on our street corners would get into hot arguments. Some said, "Hitler's actions will lead to war. You watch; he'll be annexing Holland next." Most thought differently. "If we stay neutral, we'll have nothing to fear. Besides, one of these days he'll go too far, and then he'll have France to deal with."

But I was only thirteen years old and could quickly forget the worries of other people. The only worry I had was finishing my chores, which were increasing by the day. Dad's decorating business was still doing all right. In fact, he had hired two extra men. Life was good. The aristocrats in Holland did not yet feel the pinch that most of Europe was experiencing. Mother, an excellent seamstress, was sewing for five girls and also creating all the draperies sold in Dad's business.

Saturday was a day off, and the housewives would go to the market with wicker baskets on their hips. All week long, the market area was clean and well scrubbed. But come Saturday morning at 4 A.M. things would change. The vendors would arrive in horsedrawn wagons and motor trucks. The men had built wooden stalls on the side of their wagons so everything could be sold fresh, right from the wagon. Baked goods, vegetables, fresh fish, smoked eel, and even pots and pans were for sale. It was a lively place where constant bidding was going on for these fresh goods. *"Een bloemetje voor moeder, mevrouw"* ("Take home some flowers for Mother."), the flower salesman would yell until five or six people stopped. They waited for a good price, because no home in Holland was complete or respectable without flowers on the table on Saturday night.

In the afternoon, with all the shopping done, Mother would lay out a frilly dress for each of us

43

five girls. Saturday afternoons were reserved for visiting our many relatives. Sometimes we would visit Oom Jan and Tante Dore, who lived way over on the other side of town, across the two bridges that separated Rotterdam South from the rest of the town. We would go by streetcar, and Mother and Dad took turns pointing out interesting sights. In the harbor we saw the huge ocean liners with two, sometimes three smoke stacks. "Those are the noise-makers we sometimes hear in the middle of the night," my father explained.

"And that's Holland's only airplane carrier in the middle of the Maas River. It's designed to act as a floating, movable airport. See all the airplanes there on the deck! They take off and land on the carrier, dropping a tail hook that catches one of three cables stretched across the deck. That way, they can stop in a shorter distance than they do on land." To me, it seemed like a mother hen with her chickens. You could also see the big oil refinery from Shell Oil.

There were huge grain silos with their big hoses hanging like elephants' trunks into long ships waiting to be filled with grain. These ships came from all over Europe. They had two living quarters on them, one at each end of the ship. The larger one, at the rear, was for the owner of the ship and his family. The smaller apartment, on the front, was for his helper and family. Many of these grain and ore boats were going to and fro at full speed. On them hung washlines filled with clothes. Babies were in playpens on the decks. Often we saw cats or dogs basking in the river sun.

We had plenty of stories to tell when we finally found the home of our aunt and uncle. We filled the otherwise quiet home with much laughter and many stories. They would get out the cookie box, and we would each select one and have a glass of lemonade. Then Uncle would say, "Tell us what you saw on your trip here."

All fighting to get the first word in, we would tell about the bridge that opened for the boat to pass through and how we had to wait for almost half an hour and "Uncle, you should have seen the airplane carrier!"

When finally all was excitedly explained, we were told, "Now watch quietly through the window so the adults can talk." Aunt Dore lived three stories high in a corner apartment overlooking a busy intersection. Beneath us criss-crossed bicycles, horse-drawn wagons, streetcars, and people by the hundreds. It was such fun to watch them all go by, to listen to the exciting, street sounds, and to see people doing their window-shopping or their visiting. There was so much to see that before we had seen it all, it was time for us to head for home.

In the middle of the night, I woke up to the sounds of two ocean liners. One must have been entering the harbor as the other was leaving, and they sounded their giant horns in greeting as they passed. I had heard them "blowing their stacks" before, but after seeing those big boats, I understood the difference.

On the following Friday, Mother was ready to go to prayer meeting. "I'll be leaving, girls, as soon as your father gets here. I want you to behave; I don't want to waste my time worrying about you." She had been looking forward to something special at the meeting that night. Dad had a job on the other side of town and did not come home to eat supper with us, but that was not unusual. However, this time it was getting later and later, and still he had not arrived. "Where *is* that man?" Mother kept muttering. The two youngest ones were already asleep. Nellie, Tine, and I were putting a puzzle together, but with little success; we were sharing Mother's nervousness about Father's whereabouts. We already had our nightgowns on, and still we heard no sound of Dad's footsteps. Mother walked back and forth to the window to see if she could spot him on either side of the street, but without success. He was not a man who would let Mother wait on her only night off, and a special one at that! There was no way to reach him. Everything was ready, and now this. "Probably one of those talkative customers is detaining him," Mother said.

She had at least a twenty-five-minute walk to the church, so I urged her to leave. "We'll be all right. I am a grown-up thirteen-year-old, and Dad will soon be home." Mother never bothered much with the neighbors, so she felt she couldn't ask them. "Please, Mother, go. We will be all right," I urged again.

Reluctantly she decided to go and gave me last-minute instructions. "Make sure your sisters go to bed by eight o'clock. And while you're waiting, clean their shoes. Yours, too." She forever regretted her decision to leave before Dad got home.

Soon after she was gone, I walked over to the window to look for my father. I had heard a noise. My eyes grew big with fear, for there was my Dad leaning against the wall for support as he reached for the doorknob. His face was ashen. I ran to open the door and helped him inside. "Father, Father, what's wrong?" He collapsed inside the closed door at the bottom of the five steps in the narrow hall. There was no way I could get help, because no one could even get through the door he lay behind. I called loudly for Nellie to come. Dad was conscious but gasping for air. With the full strength of our young bodies, eight-year-old Nellie and I somehow got him up those five steps and into bed. Nellie then ran next door to get help. Before any help could arrive, my father was dead.

The babies awakened because of all of the commotion and screamed loudly; Nellie and Tine were hysterical; and I was bewildered and grief-stricken. I was unable to move. I sat next to the bed looking at my father's lovely, now strangely quiet face. I tried to shake him; it could not be true. I just sat there motionless with the children screaming until Mother returned. She was with a friend. Soon neighbors were alarmed; the house filled with people and confusion. An ambulance took my father away. It still did not dawn on me that I wouldn't see him again, *ever.*

Mother's friend from the prayer meeting took matters into her own hands. I am sure she was sincere, but she never for a moment took time to help me cope with the intense grief overwhelming me. When she spoke I seemed to be hearing from far away; Dad's face was constantly before me. She told me, "*At least* help me with your sisters. Here, put your sister's socks on her while I help the little one . . . no, no, don't go near that bedroom, your mother is resting. That poor woman cannot be bothered. Here, stop your crying; give the little one her bottle so she will not wake your mother."

Finally I was allowed to go to bed, where my tears could flow freely. I wanted to see my Dad and hear him tell me that it was all right and only a bad dream. From pure exhaustion, I fell asleep without anybody ever noticing the turmoil going on within me. The sight of that ashen face kept running through my mind along with the guilty feeling that if I would only have reached a doctor, Daddy would not have died. I awoke in the middle of the night and vomited over and over again. Everyone was exhausted and no one ever noticed. My mother was behind that closed door, and I was not to disturb her. Dad was gone. Who would care about me now?

I woke up the next morning at the sound of the babies' crying, but I could not eat; I was in shock. I overheard someone say, "Keep her busy, that's the best thing to do." In a big confused family, that was not hard. So on went the instructions.

"Give your sister her bottle."

"Wash her face."

"Your sister's spoon fell; get her another."

More people came, all hovering over Mother, sympathizing with her but seemingly not with me. They would kiss the small ones and tell me, "From now on, *help your mother.*" "*Help your mother!*" "*Help your mother!*" The words echoed in my ears. I hated people—everyone!

Some spoke about God, that it must have been His Will. Absurd! His Will? I needed my dad more than God did! "O God," I cried, "Why would you do this? Why my dad? Who will help me now with Mother's moods? I do not want to live either!" I slammed my fist into the pillow wet with tears. "Why! He was too young to die. O God, nobody cares—only my dad! O Daddy—Daddy—Daddy!"

Some said, "God must have had better plans for him." What plans could He ever have had? I pictured God as cruel, punishing me for not getting a doctor in time. When I finally saw my mother again, I saw the same woman I knew from years back, again filled with bitterness. My own confused mind did not recognize that she was a widow now, with five young children to raise by herself. I felt only my own grief; I hated anyone to be around me or to touch me. So I was left alone. What I really needed was two warm arms—my mother's—to embrace me. I was desperate for a hug and a kiss and for reassurance that I had done all a thirteen-year-old girl could have done. I was my own enemy, but I didn't know it.

For two days streams of visitors came to comfort Mother. Dad's business acquaintances paid attention to the darling baby and the little sisters, but encountering the red-nosed hateful teenager with a "chip on her shoulder," they fled with, "Take good care of your mother; you are the oldest."

From all the relatives came the same command, "Take care of your mother . . . watch the babies . . . be a good girl." Over and over I heard these words and wished everyone would just go away. I was sick enough, vomiting every bite that I ate. Finally, it was all over. We laid Dad to rest in a small cemetery near the lake he loved so much. I even came to resent him. Why did he leave me with Mother? Could he not have stayed? A deep bitterness welled up in my troubled mind about the whole world and about God.

If I only had known the love of Jesus, His compassionate love. I had *learned* about Him at the Christian school, but I did not *know* Him. No one seemed to find time to sit down to get this message across to me. I was confused, bewildered, heartbroken, and horribly alone.

6

Turning My Back on God

Darkness had closed in on our once-happy family.
Who would have expected a man so young to die so
suddenly? The day after the funeral, Mother stayed
in bed with a terrible headache. She mumbled,
"Take your sisters to school with you and come right
home at twelve o'clock."

It was hard for me to meet my friends, not knowing whether they had heard. But before I got to
school, the teacher had explained it all and had
asked them to be extra kind to me. Unaware of this,
I was overcome by their kindness. It caused my
tears, which had been choked back for several days,
to start again. I wanted to stop crying, but I could
not, so I was sent home. It was no better there. The
little ones understandably felt neglected and kept
crying, which brought the past back to my mind.
Without friends and neighbors consoling her, Mother was sinking back into lapses of deep depression.
There were no visitors now, and I certainly could
have used someone. Someone's warmth and understanding. Only the doctor made regular visits. His
words to this thirteen-year-old were simply, "Keep
your chin up; it soon will get better."

Had we only known about the care Jesus gives, it
would have given Mother power to rely on, and it
would have made our future look brighter. Did not

the Bible teach that Jesus cares and that we are of great value to Him? But I saw nothing but darkness, because I did not know Him personally. Nor did my mother, despite her attendance at prayer meetings. So we were in the deepest darkness, unable to push back the agony that followed. Ironically, Mother and I felt the same, but neither of us could feel free to share our depression with the other.

The next day I went back to school, but as soon as someone as much as looked at me, the tears came again. My frustrated teacher sent me to the principal. It was a very frightened girl that entered the office of that important-looking man. I am sure he had good intentions and thought he was being helpful. I even thought he smiled at me, but I could have been mistaken. He sat down in front of his impressive desk and talked about God: "We must not question His wisdom. The Bible tells us that He works in mysterious ways. That means that He has the right to do with anyone as He sees fit."

I made up my mind then that I would not have anything to do with a God who did not care! I would never, ever want to become a Christian. Throughout all that lecture, my tears never stopped. I was asked to "Stop that crying, or I'll call your mother." I certainly did not want *her* to come; she'd only make things worse! They brought me water to drink, but even that kindness brought more tears. So my mother was summoned after all.

I'll never forget the moment she entered that office. How I wanted to cry, "Hold me!" How I wish she would have wrapped me in her arms and told me that it had not been my fault that Dad had died. Instead, after a whispered conversation with the principal, she took hold of my shoulder and in desperation said, "Now you stop that crying. You are as

51

sensitive as your father was. You'll never make it in this world; you have to become hard and tough." She glared down at me in her own determination to follow that advice. At the look on her face and the sound of her voice, I was so scared that I did not cry again until many years later.

Thereafter, on the outside I seemed to be in control, but inside I faced a raging storm. I became the big bad wolf to my sisters, and to my mother, an impossible teenager. Life was miserable without the pleasantness of Dad, without hearing his footsteps or his encouraging words. And I thought, "If there really *is* a God, He must know that I cannot live happily without my dad." Slowly, both Mother and I came to accept the inevitable. He was never to return. In time, I became "hard and tough," just as Mother had advised me. At home with Dad gone I did not care any more that one or another sister was in tears. Mother wanted me to be "hard and tough," but she didn't know how hard and tough I could become.

Teachers began to complain about my behavior, because I became a disturber in class in every way possible. I did not care to listen or to do the homework. It was the rule that in punishment a student had to write five hundred times: "I shall not disturb the class any more." After school, I waited until I had turned the corner, then I picked out some small kid from the fifth grade, handed him my punishment sheet, and told him he'd better have it finished by tomorrow morning or I would beat him up. "And you better not tell your parents or anyone else, or you will be sorry." I made many enemies in the next few months.

After selling Dad's contracts, paying off the hired men, taking care of the bills, and selling eveything,

52

my poor mother was left with only a small widow's pension. If only she had shared her heartache and worries with me, it would have been so much easier for both of us. But she would not allow anyone to mention the past. She had no room for anyone and kept her distance. She was very hard to please and almost impossible to live with. But so was I.

We soon had to look for cheaper living quarters, which meant moving closer to the harbor and the inner city. It was a humiliating experience for Mother, who had always lived in comfort. The apartment recommended by a friend was above a beauty salon where the owner once lived. He had moved and closed the entranceway from the apartment to the beauty salon. Left behind was the imprint of his affluence. On the railing of the stairway, there were large, rich-looking copper knobs. The outer door held a shiny copper knocker and a matching mail slot. It set that house apart from the very common houses on our street. It also reminded all of us of our home by the lake. For the many years we were to live there, that copper would be polished and shined weekly.

Unlike Mother, I was glad to move to new surroundings. It made it easier to put some of those bad memories behind me. But I had to share one bedroom with three sisters. Little children can be thoughtless and mean. My sisters knew that Mother and I could not get along. So they took double advantage of that situation and teased me unmercifully. At night after our bedroom door had closed, they would wait until I was almost asleep. Then they would pull my hair or pinch me and when I, half asleep, sat up suddenly, they would roll over laughing. I would jump out of bed and hit them. The result was their loud screaming—"Mother, she is hitting us again!" Mother would rush up with the rug beater and beat me instead of them. She never asked who started the trouble; *that* she took for granted. When the door closed again, Tine and Nellie would start their snickering again. I had to learn not to lose my temper. I would have given anything for some privacy, even a closet. The apartment had only two bedrooms looking out on the backs of hundreds of other apartments, all with washlines and crying children. After living in wide open spaces, I felt that the world was closing in on me. There was no time for recreation. There were always more clothes to wash and to hang and to iron. I was always tired and much too skinny.

Slowly, I found friends from the other apartments in the neighborhood, all teenagers like me in need of the basic necessities of life as well as a place of privacy where they could be themselves—a place to communicate the feelings of their age. Sunday was the only chance we had to get together. It became a habit just hanging around and going for walks. It was not a very desirable thing for a young person, but I had to identify with someone. My friendships with such teenagers developed in spite of the fact that Mother disapproved. But then, she disapproved about everything I was connected with.

Many of the homes were crowded beyond words. With the jobless situation, more and more grown brothers and sisters returned to their parents' tiny homes. Overcrowding made everyone unreasonable and cranky. Many fathers escaped their dreary existence in the nearest bar and so were glad when their teenagers were gone. Nobody missed them. Everyone had problems and nobody cared. Like many others, I had a "so what?" attitude.

My clothing was another problem. I was getting

skinnier all the time from hunger. There was not a night that I went to bed without stomach cramps. From my mother's small pension, there was no money for clothes, and her sewing jobs were dwindling. She felt very fortunate to still have her good sewing machine. Dad had kept it in good repair. Just the previous winter he had painted it shiny black. Even the Singer trademark had been given a coat of gold paint. It was a priceless possession that Mother cherished in those years of hardship. She could easily use second-hand adult clothes to sew dresses for my four little sisters, but what could she do with a skinny, tall teenager?

Help did come in the form of state aid to the poor. It must have cost Mother many sleepless nights to get up enough courage to go to the inner city to apply for assistance. She took me along. In anticipation of getting new clothes, I was really excited. But my joy was short-lived, for I soon learned I was to receive the uniform of the city's poor. I had seen kids wearing those clothes before, but I never understood why. I got two standard dresses: one blue plaid and one red plaid. Two pairs of thickly knitted long black stockings and ugly solid black shoes completed my new attire. I was supplied a pair of steel-rimmed round glasses, totally opposite of what was in fashion; they never fit my nose correctly. When I was completely adorned, I saw in the mirror my thin reflection topped with straggly, straight blonde hair. There was hate in my blue eyes. I was so ashamed!

I hated the world, the system, and my mother. I was not concerned with what she was feeling; I only knew the pain I felt. So many hard feelings could have been prevented if our family, in love, could have talked it out and prayed over it. But such thoughts never entered my twisted mind. How fortunate a family is when, in times of extreme hardship, Christ is made a part of daily living.

After being back in school for several days and wearing those despised clothes, I begged my mother, "Please, please take me out of that school! I hate it!" But it was now my turn to be punished. For a long time, I had picked on some rich kids to write my homework assignments, for they would never fight in their pretty clothes. But now the snickering started. They pointed at me.

"Do you like Nettie's new dress?"

"Is it not darling?"

"And what about those stockings? I like black, don't you?"

The relentless teasing of those schoolmates caused me anger and deep despair. Finally, on my fourteenth birthday, Mother agreed that I could leave school and find a job. It was obvious to her that my schooling was a lost cause. Besides, we needed more family income, and I was the only one old enough to help.

Down the street was a large elegant home where Mr. Van Es, a wealthy executive, lived with his family. Mother heard that Mrs. Van Es was searching for a young girl to be a mother's helper. The light work of dusting and ironing as well as helping with the cooking and other household chores was certainly something I could do. I went over to the big house by myself and was immediately received by Mrs. Van Es, a lovely woman with beautiful white hair. "You must be Nettie," she smiled. "Come in. Sit over there while I get the tea and cookies." When she returned with the tea and a plate full of still-warm cookies, she said, "Tell me about yourself, and why you quit school." She listened intently, and then hired me on the spot. Kindness was as natural to her as meanness was to me. She never had a daughter, so she immediately took me into her warm heart. Soon I was a devoted listener to anything she said. There was nothing I would not have done for her.

The Van Es home became my second home. When my work was completed, Mrs. Van Es would teach me all the things that I would otherwise have learned in school. Before her marriage, she had been a college home economics teacher, and she wanted to teach me all she knew. What had been like pulling teeth for my mother I was willing to learn for Mrs. Van Es. I was hired to work from nine until three, but I began staying longer and longer. I had the freedom to use their library. At first Mrs. Van Es selected the books for me, mostly biographies about people who had made it in spite of difficult circumstances. I had always been an avid reader and devoured anything in print.

Through careful guidance, she was developing my mind and helping me to believe what she told me over and over again: "You can go as high as you want to go." Those words were hard for a girl with such low self-esteem, dressed in the clothing of the poor, to understand, but she was changing all that. She inspired me to read all I could. If the previous night had been extra difficult and my face was sad, Mrs. Van Es would give me tea and cookies. They worked like magic. What a lovely person she was. Her friendly, smiling face and kind ways made me soon forget. How she tried to make me open up, but I didn't confide in her because if she told, Mother would send me to work somewhere else. I could not bear that thought.

Mrs. Van Es also taught me fine embroidery and

tiny handstitching for sewing my own clothes. I learned how to make jam and to can vegetables. Without really being aware of it, I was receiving a priceless education from this loving woman. I was so eager to learn. She had two sons, one two years younger than I. After he came home from school, I was asked to help him with his homework. I'm not sure who was helping whom, because he explained to me how his lessons were taught in his high school. We were good friends, and he became like a brother to me.

When the housework was finished, I had to help cook the dinner. Somehow cooking was never my specialty, but I was so dedicated to pleasing this wonderful woman, I was willing to try anything.

It was difficult when Friday came. The agreement with my mother was that I would work just five days, and not on weekends. Loaded with the thickest book I could find on the shelf, I went home feeling as though there were lead in my shoes. And not just from the weight of the books. I would read from that book in every spare moment at home, trying to escape my surroundings in the history of others.

In addition to my paycheck, Mrs. Van Es would hand me a little extra money for a pair of shoes or whatever I needed. But instead of letting me spend the money on my needs, Mother used it for food for the family. "You cannot be so selfish when the family's needs come first!" It wasn't long before Mrs. Van Es ceased to give me the extra money. Instead, *she* bought me the much-needed new shoes. Mother always frowned on her for not paying me enough. Perhaps if she had known how much I learned from Mrs. Van Es, she would have been happy for me, too. But communications with Mother were at a complete standstill.

I only tried to exist at home, for there was no other way out. The few words I spoke were rarely nice ones. I hated everyone there! Far from being an easy daughter myself, I was always trying to reform my sisters; I criticized them constantly, and they in turn teased me relentlessly. Life at home was a nightmare.

Come Monday morning, off I went to my second home. After doing the many Monday morning chores, we would stop for an eleven o'clock break. I had to get the book that I had read the past weekend and report the complete story to Mrs. Van Es. Then I would get a new book. She was as pleased with me as I was devoted to her. She continually told me, "My silver never shone so beautifully," or "The rooms never looked so cheerful. Bravo, Nettie." Placing little containers with flowers here and there, I learned the art of flower arranging.

Mrs. Van Es was thorough in all her ways. She had an air about her that made you not expect an answer to questions she did not wish to answer. She never spoke a word of criticism about my family or home. And I tried my hand at anything she encouraged, yet despite her many kindnesses, she kept her distance. Perhaps she didn't want me to think of her as a substitute for my mother. Even though she filled many of my needs, there was still an emptiness that no one filled.

So I spent more and more weekends with those newfound friends that nobody approved of. They used foul language. Their attitudes were unacceptable. They were loud, and you could see their "who cares" attitudes on their faces. But what did I care? Irresponsibility was in many ways "comfortable" to me; everywhere else I had to be on my best behavior.

They knew no kindness. We all tried to exist— some had drunken parents; some had problems like mine. All were hungry, and most of them could not find work. The only way I fit in was that I had a sense of mean humor. They could laugh until their bellies hurt. The day we passed by one of the big cathedrals, I went to a nearby store and bought a tiny bag with a few cents' worth of powdered bluing. While they stood watch, I deposited it right before mass into the holy water container. The sight of the blue-faced churchgoers from our hiding place was hilarious to us, but that day the police almost caught us. What would become of such a girl as I? I was forever searching to fill that empty cold spot deep inside of me. On the outside, in the eyes of my friends, I was strong and daring, but when I was alone, I searched vainly for a meaning to life.

7

A Friend Who Sticketh Closer Than a Mother

The pain of losing my father, the harsh feelings between Mother and me, and the new friends that even Dad would not have approved of, made my teen years a disaster. I ran farther and farther away from all the teachings of my youth. For several years, I had not entered a church (except for my prank with the bluing in the holy water). Nor had I prayed. I do not remember if I had completely done away with God, but I certainly was far away from ever wanting to be a Christian.

It happened on a Sunday evening. A dozen or so of my newfound friends had spent some hours together with me. We would have gladly stopped somewhere for food or gone to the movies, but we did not have the money. Most of us were fleeing troubled homes. All had more or less accepted the same idea that nobody cared, and we were on our own.

On that particular Sunday, it was almost dark when a sudden heavy rainstorm soaked our thin clothing. We hastily sought shelter under the overhanging roof of a building where a Salvation Army meeting was in progress. Our loud giggling and talking was probably disturbing the people inside. The door was opened by a gentleman in Salvation Army uniform. He invited us to come in. "Well—" we reasoned, "why not? Maybe we can find some fun in there. Maybe even some food." Noisily, we followed him; after all, we had to make an impression, even if a negative one. We rather enjoyed shocking people.

Inside, we saw rows and rows of long benches with about a hundred people sitting there. Most of them turned and smiled at us as we entered. We did not smile back. *Who are they grinning at?* I thought. *They don't know me.* We were all seated in one row half-way toward the front. Then the service continued. A small brass band of ten to twelve men and women played lustily. A choir of about twenty-five people, all in the familiar navy blue uniform of the Army, sang later. We had so many new things to observe that we had no time to be mischievous. We just listened and watched.

Then came the time for everyone to sing together. To our surprise, it was a melody of a street song, "Two eyes so blue, looking at you." Devilishly, knowing very well that they must have other words to that melody, we sang as loudly as possible those "street" words we knew so well. The music was stopped in the midst of the singing, and we were kindly handed songbooks with the correct words.

Those people were different. They were not stuffy "know-it-alls." They accepted us as teenagers in need of a Savior, whether we acknowledged Him or not. They were a happy bunch. They seemed to be truly sincere.

Then the preaching began, but I certainly was not going to listen to some preacher! I leafed through the songbook and closed my inner ears. Suddenly, the choir began to sing softly, and an invitation was given. That was another new thing for me. Up on the platform a woman with a lovely face stood up.

She walked down the aisle and I followed her with my eyes, wondering what she was up to. She stopped at the row where we were sitting. She politely asked my friend on the end to move over, and then the one next to her. One by one she got my friends to move until she sat down right next to me. I thought, "What did I do? Is she mad at me maybe?" Instinctively I recoiled.

But she put her arm around me—yes, she put her arm around me! Nobody would ever do that, not even my closest friend. My main weapon was my toughness. *Love* I did not give to anyone, and *love* I did not expect from anyone. I had more or less done away with the word *love.* I was respected as the most daring girl and also admired for it, but now this woman had her arm around me—not quite the situation a tough girl would choose to be in! I tightened my thin shoulders.

She asked, "What is your name?"

"Nettie."

"Nettie, I love you, and Jesus does too!"

That was too much for me. Abruptly, with bravado, I stood up, and my friends followed me out of that place. How we laughed and giggled about that "crazy woman!" We carried on about the incident, but I wanted to forget the whole thing.

But that night I could not sleep. I heard a lovely voice saying over and over, "Nettie, I love you, and Jesus does too!" The following day at work was lonely. No one was around. Mrs. Van Es was at the hospital where her ailing husband had been taken that weekend. In the stillness of that day, I could not rid myself of that voice. How maddening it was! For the next three weeks, I heard her voice over and over, and I began to reason with that little voice within me. It could not *be* that Jesus loved *me.* If Jesus really existed, then God must exist too. The pain from the loss of Dad returned to my mind. So early in life I had had to give him up just when I needed him the most.

But a longing started. What if—what if it really *was* true, that there *was* a God who cared? I quickly shoved the idea out of my mind as an impossibility. Who was I, a confused, hateful teenager, that God, the Maker and Creator of the universe, should care about what happened to me? And again, I pushed the thought out of my mind, only to be reminded of the lovely voice, "Nettie, I love you, and Jesus does too!" I started wondering, *Who was that woman, anyhow? Will she be there every Sunday night, or was she a guest that evening? Who in the world is she?* I was going to find out.

The following Sunday, I told the whole gang, "Let's go back and see if that crazy woman is still there."

"Yeah," they said, with the devil in their eyes.

I took things in hand, "You'd better not try anything you'll be sorry about later. You" —I pointed to Terry—"sit at my left and you, Ria, on my right. You two better stay there and don't move, or else." I had enough reputation for them to heed my warning.

We arrived a little earlier than we had the first time so we would be there from the start. Again, we were seated in the same row, only it was more crowded. At the end of each bench they had placed a person instructed to pray throughout the service. I only found that out later.

We were overwhelmed by the friendliness of the people. It was as though we did *them* a favor in coming. Glancing at the choir, I saw the woman I sought, the face of my affliction. She didn't see me, or so I thought. I felt safe with the knowledge that she could never get to me this time. Again, I was enticed by the happy atmosphere I was not familiar with. But I was not at ease anymore. The more the meeting progressed, the more uneasy I felt. How foolish, I reasoned, to have come back! I began to plan how to get out of this situation. But how do you handle friendliness and kindness? And for the first time I realized I had to stay and face a decision that was confronting me. I could not just stand up and leave, even if I wanted to. What was the matter with me? It was maddening!

In the band, there was an Army lassie with a tambourine in her hand, and she rattled and banged it so happily that my attention was temporarily directed toward her. I would not mind trying to play that thing once. The choir sang, and I tried to hide behind the man in front of me so that the source of my affliction on the platform would not detect me.

Finally the preaching started; I consoled myself that it soon would be over and I would be out of there. I kept my mind so occupied that in no time flat, the preaching stopped and the choir began to sing. Suddenly that woman stood up. My friends started snickering, but I was shaking. Again I instructed my friends on the left and right not to move. I knew she could never get into our row because it was already so crowded, but down the aisle she came. The man on the end stood up, and she quickly moved past him and past all my friends. Only my stubborn friend seated next to me was left, but the woman grabbed her and planted her squarely on the opposite side. Instantly I knew that I could not handle this situation.

Kindly and so serenely the Salvation Army woman spoke. "Nettie, I love you, and Jesus does too!"

I started to cry my heart out. That made me so angry. I had not shed a tear for many years. I looked at her and said, "Jesus does not love me, and God doesn't either; otherwise my father would not have died—he was too young—he was the only one who really understood me."

For a moment no one spoke. Then the woman said, "Nettie, I do not know why God took your father away so early in his life, but I know one thing for sure: if you had been the only person on this earth, God would have sent His only Son to die for you on the cross, so you could have His forgiveness and eternal happiness."

"How do you know that?" I asked.

"Well, Nettie," she explained, "it is in the Bible." Then she opened her Bible and read from John 3:16. "For God so loved [Nettie], that He gave His only begotten Son, that [if Nettie] believes in Him [she will] not perish, but have eternal life."

There it was in black and white, and it sounded pretty convincing. I asked, "What can I do about it? I have really tried to change many times, but I couldn't. I am angry at everyone; I hate my mother the most. I do not know how to get out of such a mess."

Tenderly she answered, "Nettie, if you give your heart and life to Jesus Christ, He will teach you to love and to forgive. He gives new longings in your heart and new desires. Why don't you stand up, come forward with me to the altar, kneel down, and give your heart and life to Jesus? Ask His forgiveness, and He will give it to you."

"You mean stand up here, in front of all my friends?"

"Yes, Nettie," she replied. Then she quoted from Isaiah 53:3, 5: " 'He was despised and forsaken of

66

men. . . . He was pierced through for our transgressions.' He died on the cross for you."

Slowly I stood up. I saw that the meeting had ended and that my friends had left me, but I also saw people kneeling everywhere praying for my soul. I shed bitter tears at that altar that Sunday. What a joy to find forgiveness and new life! The Bible says the angels in heaven rejoice over one sinner saved by the blood of Jesus, who was now my Savior. I knew that now life was going to be worth living. What a difference from the bitterness I had felt only an hour earlier!

I went home jubilant that night, sure that this time my mother would be very proud and pleased with me. Upon reaching the house, I hurriedly ran up the stairs to find her already asleep. Softly I woke her up. Kneeling by her bedside, I told her about the great decision that I had made. I wanted to love her, but she did not understand, and I saw again what a great disappointment I was to her.

She sat up in bed. "Honestly, Nettie, what did you do now? Why did you even go there? That's the gathering place for the down-and-outers. Were you looking for a boyfriend, maybe? Yes, that would be next, a daughter married to a drunk. And what is this talk that your sins were forgiven? That's not that easy, you know. Why don't you go with me to our church this Sunday and *prove* to me that you've changed?" Disgusted, she turned over on her side, mumbling "Salvation Army—a rescue place for drunks—sins forgiven, huh?"

As I rose from my knees, anger welled up in me. But for the first time, I felt sorry for Mother, because I knew that she needed the same happiness as I had found. I wish I could say I loved her unconditionally from that time on, but that was not so. It was to take years. Many times I felt angry and hopeless. I was very hard on myself for not being able to love as I should. Then I realized that only with the help of God, my heavenly Father, would I overcome my feelings toward my family.

The day after my big decision, I told Mrs. Van Es about it. She listened carefully and then said, "That was a good choice, but I am afraid that you are in for a most difficult time. Your friends will probably leave you." I could not believe that. She went on talking, trying to find a solution to my problem. "Get in touch with the officers of that same Salvation Army Corps. There must be plenty of work to do. And show your family that you really have changed. Eventually they will realize it and believe you." That day when I sat down to eat lunch, I bowed my head for the first time to pray for a blessing on that food, and it was as though my Dad were saying, "Now you're on the right track."

After work that evening, I wanted to go and speak about the future with the people of the Salvation Army, but first I went to the street corner where my friends were hanging around. Instead of greeting me as usual, they stared at me as though I came from another planet. Henk was the first one who scornfully said, "So you got religion last night, eh?" Rolling his eyes heavenward and making a screeching sound he asked, "Anyone else who wants religion?" They started laughing and shaking their heads. Turning away from me he said, "Not me, either."

I stood there hurt and lonely with tears in my eyes. I felt like running after them, but it was as though Someone held me back. I could not follow them. Slowly I made my way to the Salvation Army hall. Somehow, a weight had been lifted from my shoulders.

8

Slum Work with the Salvation Army

During the next several weeks, things were slowly changing. First of all, my mother must have seen my honest effort. My sisters still played the same game that had made me so angry. One night when the relentless teasing began again, I got up, put on my clothes, and pushed my two sisters in front of me and down the steps to my mother, who was reading a book. They were scared and tried to get away by whining and crying. I told my mother how many times I had been punished for things *they* did and that I was just tired of being awakened by their pulling my hair and by all the other pranks. Mother asked them in surprise, "Did you do that?" They naturally denied it, but from that day on they never woke me up again. That was a welcome change, but not everything went so well. I had lost my friends. I felt intensely lonely.

One day someone told me that I was to go to see the captain of the Salvation Army. Hurrying on, I wondered why she had called for me. I rang the bell to her apartment near the Salvation Army hall. The lieutenant who had led me to the Savior opened the door quickly. She kissed me and invited me into the living room, where they had tea ready. I did not know what they wanted of me, so I skipped the tea and asked them to explain why they had called me. They said, "Nettie, you indicated that you wanted to become a soldier. There's no time like the present. So why not this Sunday? We've found a uniform that will fit you to a 'T.' The only thing you have to buy is black stockings."

"Well," I thought, "who would ever have thought that I would go out of my own free will and buy black stockings?" I felt extremely happy to become a full-fledged member of the Salvation Army. I sat there that evening explaining the change that had taken place in me in the last months. I did not talk about the struggles with Mother. Somehow I felt ashamed that I was unable to cope with her. But I gladly accepted the invitation to become a Salvation Army soldier.

I went back home to tell Mother and ask her to come to the ceremony, but she would not even think of it. Such a position was below our family dignity, to her way of thinking. And so that Sunday morning I went alone, dressed up in the mercy uniform of the Salvation Army. I took my oath solemnly. On each side of my collar, the lieutenant pinned a shiny copper "S," standing for the motto: *Saved to Serve.* I also got a little black Bible. Standing under the red, yellow, and blue flag of the Salvation Army, I pledged my life to Jesus Christ, who by His grace saved me and gave Himself up for me.

After I had completed my oath, I was immediately pressed into service, and serving others soon became my second nature. I was given a small Sunday school class of five to eight children to be taught every Sunday morning at nine o'clock. An older soldier listened in for a few weeks to make sure I did my teaching properly. I had been blessed with a love for kids, and storytelling seemed to delight them. I prayed with them frequently; I felt it such a great responsibility. Now all the learning from the strict Christian school of my earlier life aided me greatly. After a few weeks, I became an accredited Sunday school teacher.

As time passed, I realized that my past behavior and the desires I formerly had were slowly being replaced by far better ones. The Army gave me a new opportunity, a new life: working with the children in the slum area of Rotterdam. As it was throughout the world, so it was in Rotterdam; the inner city had become overcrowded and given birth to a vast amount of tragedy.

In many taverns, people were filling themselves with the false happiness of alcohol. Those alcoholics totally neglected their offspring. The children were not adequately dressed, fed, or loved. At a time of great need for love in my own life, I was brought into *their* love-starved lives. How they would sit and listen to the stories I had learned in earlier years in the Christian school! It was like a golden thread of God's care, woven and extended to those children. I learned to love them, although they were poorly clad, often dirty, and always had running noses (a sight I never got used to). The Salvation Army uniform had huge side pockets. Inside one pocket I would carry half a roll of toilet paper, for tissues were unknown, to wipe the ever-running noses of the slum children. Into my other pocket went the used toilet paper until I could find an emptying receptacle.

Cleanliness was a necessary lesson for the children under such desperate conditions. They were so hungry to learn, just for the reward of a smile. Not only was it medicine for their hungry hearts, but it taught me gratitude for my own home and clean bed. I often had the opportunity to visit in the slum homes, because the uniform of the Salvation Army was widely accepted as a trademark of mercy. The first thing one noticed was the mixed smell of urine and alcohol. Then between boxes and trash one might see a bed often shared by four children who slept across its width. Many were bedwetters, and with no heat, the beds never really dried up.

Once we found an extremely bad case in which a mother was sick; she had five children without warm enough clothes to get out of bed, much less go outside to brave the winter cold. The father was shamelessly drunk, and I told Mrs. Van Es about it. She and some of her friends told me to take those kids to a department store so they would all have a new pair of shoes, a winter coat, and underwear. They were dressed from top to bottom. We bought the sick mother a big basket of food. Two weeks later, five crying children in old dirty clothes came into our meeting. Their drunken father had taken all their new clothes to the pawnshop in trade for alcohol. We learned our lesson with that case. But it never discouraged the Salvation Army people. They went right on, and so did I. It became my life's desire to help. How the people held on to every word of hope I read from my small Bible! I took every possible opportunity to spread God's Word to the needy.

It was a joy to *me* to be of help, even though we would sometimes find ourselves in impossible situations. We were never to enter a home if we had not first told our officers what time we entered, and we had to report back as soon as we finished our visit. If we found ourselves unable to handle any situation or felt any personal danger, we could go directly for help to our Salvation Army headquarters or to the very cooperative city officials. Very seldom, if ever, was this necessary.

The hardest job to get used to was to go into the many taverns of the inner city on Saturday night to sell *The War Cry,* the official magazine of the Army. We were instructed always to go with a partner. From afar we could hear the boisterous voices inside of the bars. The moment we opened the door, the stale tobacco smoke combined with the cheap alcoholic smell would hit us, and it was almost unbearable. Two more of our workers stayed at the door to make sure we were safe. At least one of the four in each team had to be a man. With our Bible in one hand and our *War Cry* in the other, we would show this sorrowful bunch inside that their only hope was Jesus Christ. With their tongues doubling up, they would use the foulest language toward us. They laughed at us and scorned us. It took me many more years to accept the idea that God also loves such sinners. At that time in my life I was always willing to run away from places like that.

Today, as a mother of five children myself, I can understand the worry my own mother went through, knowing where I was working. She tried everything to make me give up my beloved job. "How can you stand those horrible places, those stinking drunks? You should be out working a real job, bringing in money for your own family. Charity begins at home, you know. Look at all the hours you could work for money instead of going to bars on Saturday night." She also wanted me to go to her dignified church. I did go with her on special occasions, but I felt called to work with the least and the lost. It made Mother angry.

One day I could not stand the hassling any longer,

so I went to speak to the lieutenant, the woman with the lovely face who had introduced me to Jesus. Maybe I expected sympathy from her. Instead, she took God's Word and opened it to Exodus 20:12. She told me to read it aloud.

"Honor your father and your mother—"

"Stop," she said. "Read it again."

So I did. "Honor your father and your mother—"

"What kind of a mother?" she asked.

"What do you mean?" I questioned.

"Does it say a mother I can understand, a mother who is nice all the time, a mother without faults?"

"No," I answered, "I see nothing of that sort."

"Well," she said, "you do the honoring and loving, and God will do the changing." She hugged me and sent me back home to start following God's command.

That lieutenant was well-trained. She stayed in Rotterdam for four more weeks and then was transferred to another field of service. I missed her wisdom and kindness. She was the greatest influence in my young Christian life. But life does not stand still just because someone we care about moves on.

Sundays were busy days with many activities. In addition to the regular morning and evening services at the church where I had become a Sunday school teacher, there was an afternoon children's meeting. At four o'clock a small group of young people from the Army met together to go to the slum area of the inner city. We carried a big megaphone made of cardboard. We stopped in several locations, sang a lively song to attract the children, and then used the megaphone to announce the children's rally to commence at five o'clock in the Salvation Army hall. Mothers, hearing our announcement, would quickly dress their offspring and send them off with us. About one hundred to one hundred and fifty children of all ages would follow us back for the rally. Our progam was lively and included much singing. One of us would tell a gospel-related story similar to a parable, an earthly story with a heavenly meaning. More singing was followed by a Bible story showing the children the wonderful way Jesus could change their lives and make them new creations. I always loved to tell stories, and the children were good listeners. They also let us know in no uncertain terms how they liked our stories!

One day I was asked to start that same children's rally program on Thursdays at five o'clock. Just one other girl was able to help me, but only occasionally at that. All of the other young people had jobs at that hour. And so three months after my decision to follow Jesus, I was in charge of a children's rally. At first, the hardest part was to go and gather up all the children. It wasn't long, though, until the kids met me half-way between my house and theirs, many fighting to hold my hand or to get a smile. Others went directly to the building and waited for the program to begin. There was a set of big brothers who did their best to interrupt the program. When I made each of them a "captain" in charge of a row of smaller children, I no longer had any problem with them. Many of those children became Christians. I loved every moment of this children's ministry, and they knew it. When Jesus fills a life, He fills it to overflowing with abundant joy. I got to know lovely Christian workers, and within a short time I had a whole new set of good Christian friends.

Once a month a group of young people rode on bicycles, rain or shine, to the neighboring suburban areas to sell *The War Cry* door to door. The paper served a dual purpose: first of all it brought the loud and clear message of salvation; but also, a few cents of each copy was for our own officers' bread and butter. Although I have never heard of any of them complain, they could have. Their support was meager. And none of their other members were ever able to bring them anything extra, for we were all poor. They were dedicated—soul, heart, and body—to the cause of Christ.

Among those young people selling *The War Cry* was a young man named Jake, who began to work often within our circle of friends. He was tall and handsome, but shy. Everyone liked him. You could count on him to keep his word. If he said, "I'll be there at six," you could set your watch by his word. He was so willing to help. He never asked, "Will it take long?" or "Is it much work?" He worked at the job with all his heart. All the girls had their eyes on him, but when the work was done he would come straight to me and say, "You want to ride your bicycle home with me?" I was impresssed from the start by his solid character. I found him pleasant to be with. He was learning to play a trombone, but he had not yet become a soldier of the Salvation Army. Soon we became close friends, and looked for more and more opportunities to be together.

One day he had to pick up something at home and I waited by our two bikes. When he came down he said, "My mother wants to meet you." It took me by surprise. I quickly combed my long blonde hair, congratulating myself for wearing my new woolen dress with the wide, beautiful skirt. Afraid that it was obvious how scared I was, I entered the room where his lovely gray-haired mother sat along with his four sisters and two married brothers and so many nieces and nephews. His family was a happy bunch. Everyone joked with me, and pretty soon I felt at ease. At that stage, Jake and I were only good friends. Although my feelings may have gone a step or two past friendship, I was always worried that a draft notice would come for him. He had had his eighteenth birthday, and our country had mobilized her army. Hitler was moving Nazi troops into many countries around us. Most young men Jake's age had already been summoned. Our only comfort was that if our country remained neutral, nobody would ever touch it. What a myth that was!

A food shortage began, and many families started hoarding rice, coffee, tea, sugar, flour, and other items. It wasn't long before the entire country was uneasy, fearful about what was to come. These circumstances made it even more difficult for Mother to provide the most basic needs for our big family. Our shoes were repaired and stitched over and over again, and then handed down to the next sister when outgrown. Mother's life was hard.

Furthermore, she shared her difficulties with no one. She withdrew into herself as soon as I tried to get near. She was that way not only to me, but to everyone who honestly tried to help. I just threw myself more into the slum work, and I continued to find satisfaction in the job I still maintained with the Van Es family.

It was clear to me that I must soon find myself a better paying job. I hated to think of leaving this family that was so good to me. But no matter how I tried, I could not find another job, so I stayed on a little longer with the Van Eses. I was in charge of all the work and was very much appreciated. When I first started working for them, I ate by myself in the kitchen, but one day I was invited to sit at the dinner table with the family. This was not a Dutch custom by any means! They showed great interest in the change they saw in my life. They also asked about the Salvation Army and often came to special programs. But for the most part, they kept their distance. As in the typical European expression, I was "only a dime and never to become a quarter!" Regardless, I loved them dearly, and there was nothing I would not have done for them

Now eighteen, I was looking for employment with more challenges, but this was not to occur before some very drastic changes had taken place.

9

No Way Out

Saturday, May 10, 1940 was a sunny spring morning. The fragrance of flowering lilacs, the beauty of tulips in full bloom, and the songs of the birds all seemed in harmony with the beautiful month of May.

But from high above came the harrowing sounds of German airplanes; they had been roaring since 4:00 A.M., turning the beautiful morning into a day of deep sorrow. World War II was invading our once-peaceful country.

Our troops had been mobilized for several months. Young women like me had been trained by the Red Cross in survival tactics.

What fun it had been to bandage dummies with imaginary head and leg wounds. We never thought this training would be used for real wartime tragedies. We had been fitted for gas masks. Our first aid courses were extended. We even practiced evacuating a city in time of war. How mistaken we were not to take it seriously, for this morning plane after plane was parachuting heavy equipment and troops into the center of Rotterdam. As soon as people woke up they ran into the streets asking each other, "What is that, what's happening? Why these planes? Why the shooting?" Hurrying back to their homes, they sat close by their radios as an announcer passed on a message from our beloved Queen Wilhelmina: our country was being invaded by the German Air Force, even though Germany had promised all along not to include Holland if strict neutrality was practiced. We listened with fear and trembling to learn what the next step toward doom would be.

First, the schools were closed and taken over by the Dutch government, who filled them with their own troops, hoping to defend the city. It was an unexpected vacation for the children, but they did not play in the streets. Their chatter and noisy laughter were stilled. They all huddled close to their mothers like anxious birds. Many families joined each other for solace. Everyone worked to turn their neighborhood schools into barracks for our fighting men or into much-needed hospital space.

Between the Nazis' ground troops in the southern part of Rotterdam and their parachutists in the North was the "locked-in" Dutch marine force, far outnumbered by the well-equipped Nazi troops. We were very proud of our men, who fought valiantly to keep the two strategic bridges dividing Rotterdam from being taken by the enemy. Many fathers and young sons lost their lives defending their country.

Every able-bodied man was called to help fight the Nazis. Under the sound of heavy mortar and machine-gun fire, women, children, and old people waited things out on the lowest floor of their homes or in nearby air raid shelters. It seemed like a nightmare, but reality forced us to face the hard facts of war. Many hands were folded in prayer, and anxious tear-streaked faces were lifted to our heavenly Father in hopes that He would protect all that was dear to them. Being so abruptly pulled into an unwanted war, people began to pray as they never had before. Few slept when that Saturday ended, because the fighting continued through the night.

Sunday morning dawned quietly compared with the noisy previous day. A radio bulletin from the Dutch government had advised all citizens to make preparations for immediate evacuation. Each family member was to pack a suitcase. There was little to do but wait.

I lived just two blocks from where I taught a Sunday school class. Because it was quiet, Mother gave me permission to go to the Salvation Army building. I wondered if any children would be there. Sure enough, I found four little ones outside with pale faces and scared eyes. My arms surrounding all four children, we slipped inside and prayed together. To give them something else to think about, I told the story I had prepared for that day. It was about Moses and the Israelites, how they went through the Red Sea with enemy troops behind them and how God opened a path for them. I made it short, because machine-gun firing had started again, intensifying by the minute. We didn't know until later that our Marine headquarters had been bombed to the ground. The five of us knelt once more to pray and wondered if we would ever see each other again. I presented these children to Jesus and never saw them again. Did they lose their lives that following Tuesday along with hundreds of others?

Two days later that church was rubble. It was good we had not known what would happen, because fear would have stopped our hearts! If there was ever a country in prayer, it certainly was the small nation of Holland. All through the night we heard the relentless firing in the harbor by the Dutch Z-5 torpedo boats and the machine guns of the Dutch Marines. To keep the enemy from taking over our oil refineries in Pernis on the southern outskirts of Rotterdam, the English bombed them. We could hear those bombs as well as those that destroyed our airport. From afar we saw the heavy smoke and the brightly lit sky. We heard the roaring of the airplanes combined with the whistling sounds of falling bombs. It was hell all about us—a frightening night. Hoping against hope that it wouldn't touch us, we huddled around the radio, listening to minute-by-minute descriptions about the dreadful happenings in our city.

On Tuesday, everything was quiet, deadly quiet—not a noise was heard, not a soldier seen. The radio was playing soft music uninterrupted by newscasts. It was like the eye of a hurricane. People started to stick their heads out of the doors and windows. Quickly we checked on nearby relatives and friends.

At midmorning it was still quiet, so Mother took my four sisters to visit a friend on the next street. All the belongings we had gathered for a quick evacuation were left at the foot of the stairs, where we could easily get them if needed. Meanwhile, I went to the end of our street to say goodbye to the Van Es family. We had all planned to return home by three o'clock that afternoon. But plans made in wartime often go wrong.

The Van Es family had decided (because it was so calm) to leave that morning for the safety of their summer home in the country. Mrs. Van Es was quite worried about her husband. He was not fully recuperated from a serious ailment, but had been sent home early from the hospital because space was needed for wounded soldiers. When I arrived that day around one, they and their two teenagers were prepared to leave. Mr. Van Es's sister Rika was to stay behind until an ambulance could come to take their bedridden ninety-year-old mother to the country home. But Rika was dreadfully afraid of being left alone; so when the rest of the family left, I promised to stay with Rika and the old woman until the ambulance arrived.

They were not gone long when the sirens suddenly started their horrifying sounds again, followed almost immediately by the droning of the airplane engines and the wailing of falling bombs. Everywhere, even right across from us, homes were aflame. I hurried to the window from which I had always been able to see my own home. But now, I could not believe my eyes. There must have been a direct hit, for our home and that of our neighbors were gone. Still disbelieving, I quickly opened the window to see better but one more glimpse confirmed my fear—there was only rubble, a few smoking ruins. Plane after plane dropped its deadly cargo. Evacuation time had come. Only one thought pressed on the minds of thousands of people—to get out of the city.

Rika and I stood and watched at the window as people passed by with their belongings loaded into anything that had wheels—baby buggies, carts, bicycles. They were loaded with bedding and clothing as well as their old, their sick, and their babies. One old man carried nothing but a gray cat. The adults were frantic, and the children screamed. On both sides of the narrow streets, houses continued to burn, some set afire by wind-swept flames from other houses. Throughout the city, 26,000 homes were on fire, as were all the hospitals and twenty-seven churches. The whole city was burning. What I saw through the window was a running, pushing, terrified, screaming mass of people—some bleeding and badly wounded—trying desperately to escape the holocaust.

I prayed for wisdom. Here I was, only eighteen, in charge of Rika and her old mother, who were still so sure the ambulance would arrive any minute. Their solid old house would never fall, they thought. But when a new group of planes dropped heavier bombs and the foundation began to sway, I knew we could wait no longer. Rika became hysterical.

When I shouted that we had to move her mother, the old woman cried, "Let me die here—I haven't long to live anymore, so let me die in my own house." All I could do was pray for divine guidance and move quickly. We had to get out, *fast*. The street was empty now. So I put pillows on the dining room chair and placed the frail, crying old woman on top. Rika was shaking, almost frozen with fear, as I yelled to her to help carry her mother. As we struggled outside with our burden, the door slammed into me. The pain was very bad, but soon forgotten in the urgency of our escape.

We had to keep going, carrying Rika's mother between us, trying to keep the flying burning debris out of our hair. The rows of three-story houses on both sides of the narrow streets were afire, spewing flames from every window. Many walls collapsed, almost lazily. Here and there only a smoking heap remained from a direct hit. Rika was crying. The old woman was moaning.

Suddenly, as though from nowhere, came the ambulance, picking its way through the rubble. Mr. Van Es, a prominent man, had been able to influence that driver to come into an impossible situation. Other people had seen it as a means of escape and had crammed into every available space. They clung to the rooftop, the doors, and wherever they could grab hold. The driver stopped when he saw us with the old woman. We were able to put her safely inside. I had to push Rika in. There was absolutely no room for me. I prayed that the ambulance would not collapse from overcrowding. But it slowly pulled away, and suddenly I was alone.

My friends and my family were all gone. Out of the smoke came a policeman screaming to me, "Go back, go back, you'll burn alive." Before I could react, the thick smoke separated us again, and I was alone. I came upon one more person, a Dutch soldier leaning against a light pole with his head on his arm, crying uncontrollably. More bombs fell and I ducked instinctively. When I looked up, he too was gone. Smoke and flames were all around me. I could not breathe, and was forced to fall to the ground on my knees. I was aware that this must be the end. There was no way to escape. Yet even though I knew there was no chance for me to get out of that smoke and fire, I was completely calm. It must have been the presence of Jesus that kept me from fear.

My thoughts began to race as I prayed, "Lord, I want to live—for you!" A plan started to form in my mind. I knew where I was, and I knew that the highway leading out of the city was only a few hundred feet away—but which way? I could not remember which direction I was facing. It seemed as though my mind were a fast-unwinding reel. I could hear myself telling the story of Moses to that small Sunday school class—how God opened a path for Moses to pass through the Red Sea. I prayed, "Lord God, You are my heavenly Father. You did it for Moses; I believe You can do it for me, too. Please, Lord, make a way out!"

I was in an L-shaped street and had already come around the corner. A huge factory behind me was burning like a torch. I could hear the planes returning. A sudden dreadful fluting sound made me realize a bomb was going to hit directly behind me. The explosion caused the entire front wall of the factory to fall straight forward, blowing a path like an air tunnel right through the flames. There it was—a way out! I jumped up and ran through that space just in time as the wall of fire closed again behind me. On the main road, thousands of people were fleeing for their lives. Some who saw me come out of the flames said in disbelief and with wide eyes, "Did you come out of there?"

I told them, "God brought me out—Jesus did it!"

They only said, "Poor kid, lost her mind." Nobody believed me, because not a hair of my head was burned or even scorched. The verse in Isaiah 43:1-2 came to mind:

> . . . Do not fear, for I have redeemed you; I have called you by name, you are Mine! When you pass through the waters, I will be with you; and through the rivers, they will not overflow you. When you walk through the fire, you will not be scorched, nor will the flame burn you.

I took only a moment to stand there in awe of what had just happened, realizing the presence of God in the midst of such chaos! Then I was swept into that mob of humanity, all hurrying out of the city to the safety of the countryside.

Although it was still the middle of the afternoon, the thick smoke from the burning homes and shops made the sun look like a big dull red ball. And it seemed that evening had already come. We all walked around huge craters made by errant bombs that had burst in the street.

Suddenly the bombing stopped, almost as abruptly as it had begun. We came to the open road, where

Boy Scouts had buckets of fresh water for people to drink. Everyone sipped from the same ladle, because that was all there was. How refreshing that water was, and how grateful we were for our escape and for the sudden quiet.

The Red Cross had hastily erected stands, where they could serve soup from big kettles. Helping hands were needed, so I too started spooning soup. I worked until my legs and feet ached and I could stand no longer.

That night I slept on a bed of hay in a barn by the side of a country road. I had been unsuccessful in my attempt to find my family that evening. The children crying around me and the sobbing adults calling out for lost loved ones were almost too much for me to bear. The tears began to flow, and I cried out to my Lord for comfort. I looked up in the sky and saw just one star.

> Schittered de ster van zyn trouwe,
> In des te schoner pracht!

Translated from Dutch the hymn says, "Shines the star of His faithfulness/In ever more powerful strength!" I knew, beyond a doubt that Jesus was there, surrounding me, His child.

I owned nothing on this earth anymore. I had no family (so I thought), but through my tears I was overwhelmed by the knowledge of His presence. My heart was filled to overflowing with praise to the Lord of my salvation. Calmly I laid my head on the straw and fell asleep, sustained and secured by His everlasting arms.

10

The Search for My Family

The next morning I awoke so early that the dew had not yet evaporated. An overwhelming thankfulness came over me, mixed with anxiety about whether my mother and my sisters had survived. I wondered where I could find them and where to start looking. All around me lay people who, like me, slept wherever they could put down their heads. In those quiet moments, I commended the day to my Lord. I had come so close to death the day before that I had a new strength for living, and I voiced my reliance on the Lord. I committed my day, my hands, and all my fears to Him.

The first sound I heard came from a baby crying, followed by another. They were hungry, wet, and smelly. The slightly older toddlers were equally noisy with their crying. They did not understand what was happening, and they clung to their mothers' skirts. Despair was everywhere. Most of the men were bewildered. They had no way of providing for their families. Some farmers were setting out pails of water, and I went over to speak with them. I told them about the Red Cross emergency center not far away where they could direct these people.

I hurried to the Red Cross center myself. My training during the preceding months for this emergency evacuation was valuable now. Other volunteers and I were assigned to rope off certain areas for the mass of humanity soon to arrive. For a registration table, we turned over a large crate. I helped to organize the people into lines for food and other immediate needs. Inquiry lines were formed so that names could be recorded to help people find one another. As soon as a missing person was reported, one of the volunteers would write the name on a bulletin board that had been fastened to the side of the barn. A written list of names was passed on to the next Red Cross post, and to the next and so on, for there were many such posts. At each, a doctor was on duty to care for the sick. A separate area was roped off to care for babies. The needs of people were great, and the volunteers did their best to comfort and provide for those needs.

What a welcome sight the truckload of bread and hot coffee was when it arrived! Not everyone was cooperative. Hungry people pushed and shoved to get to the head of the line. They had been through a lot, and we workers had to be patient with them. Some were trying hard to please; others were difficult to work with. I just helped wherever there was a need. Still racing through my mind were thoughts of all the places where Mother might have left word of her survival. There were so few volunteers for so much work that I hated to leave. However, I could stand it no longer. I found the nerve to ask the head of the emergency setup if I might be spared for a few hours to search for my own family.

I was given a stamped permit to reenter the still-smoldering city. It was a long walk back, but I did not need a map because the heavily smoking ruins were visible for miles. I feared going back alone, but in such terrifying times, it seems Jesus is nearer. I felt His presence more than ever before. As I walked toward the city, I had all I owned in this world in a bag over my shoulder—a change of clothes, a few toilet articles, and a neatly wrapped cheese sandwich. I cannot remember if I was concerned or not about having absolutely nothing else but that bag; I remember only the urgency to find my family.

Right at the city limits was a barricade across the road. A shock went through me, for there in the ugly Nazi uniform complete with helmet and gun, was the first enemy soldier I was to encounter. Even though I realized the devastation about me, I had not seen a newspaper or talked with anyone about the real people involved—German soldiers. So then and there I felt the full impact of having lost to the oppressor. Hate and anger came over me, all directed toward that man who represented the misery and sorrow of everything that had happened. For a moment, I hesitated to hand him my certificate. It was only the compelling desire to find my family that kept me from turning back. I showed him my pass without even looking at him. So I was granted entrance and hurried past that one soldier, only to discover that the whole road was full of them. As I saw how triumphant they were over their newly-won territory, I became troubled both in mind and soul.

I hurried on, trying to find some familiar place. First, I came to a heap of rubble that I recognized as the place where our home had once stood. It was one thing to have seen the ruins the day before from a distance, but quite different to stand right next to it. Strangely, one wall was still standing up and way up high hung Mother's red dishpan. That's all that was left. It was no use trying to climb through all that debris to go to the Van Es home because I could see in the distance that even that stately brick house had been totally destroyed. As I looked around, I could see a chimney here and a wall over there and even part of a foundation, but there was not one single house still standing. Seeing it all was a shattering experience. Hoping to escape all of this, I went on to the street where Mother had gone. There the houses had also been destroyed—broken glass everywhere, a burned-out bus overturned. The still badly smoking debris gave off such a foul smell that I thought I would faint. Iron beams were melted into awkward shapes. The emptiness all around made the scene seem ghostly. I had to watch out constantly for collapsing walls all around. Even so, I felt compelled to search until I had found someone.

Ruins of Salvation Army Building

I wanted to see the Salvation Army building. I would not be satisfied until I saw it. And there it was—two tall steel beams rising high in the air connected by an iron crossbar, looking like an arch. As I stood and gazed at that arch, the impact of all I had seen hit me. Everywhere I looked, little fires were still consuming what was left. All the familiar places were gone. I was in a state of shock. Suddenly, I realized I should not have made this trip alone. I sat down on a stone and sobbed. Was Mother gone too? My sisters? Were any of my family and friends still living?

In my sorrow, I lost all track of time. I had been there longer than I thought. I was startled by a hand on my shoulder. Lifting my head, I looked into the kind faces of rescue workers. When I told them my worry, they advised me to go back and search the countryside. They assured me that many had survived. So I made my way back, again passing that dreadful German soldier. I hurried on; I still could not look at him.

I thought, where else to look? Then I remembered the country home of the Van Es family. It was a long walk—at least ten kilometers—or was it twenty? I was tired and discouraged, but the possibility of finding a loved one kept me going. When I got there and knocked on that door, everyone came running to let me in. In chorus, they asked if I was all right. They grasped my hands and shouted for joy. It was so good to laugh for a change. I had been convinced that all that had happened had robbed me of the gift of laughter. I was so happy that the Van Eses were all safe. Rika, crying when she saw me, said, "I thought you had died." Seeing me seemed to relieve her of the guilt feeling she felt in having to leave me behind, even though I knew there was no other way.

When I saw Rika's old mother in her clean bed, I was so grateful that we had urged and helped her to leave the city behind and that she had escaped. She lived only six more weeks, but was surrounded by her loved ones and died in peace.

Over hot tea and biscuits, I told the Van Es family all I had been through in trying to locate my mother and sisters. I also made it clear that I now had to continue my search, even though they were so kind in offering to let me stay. Mr. Van Es hugged me and said, "How could we ever repay you for seeing that Rika and Mother got here safely?" Mrs. Van Es was equally grateful. "Now listen," they said, "If you cannot locate your family, we will adopt you as our own." Even though it was meant kindly, it brought back the real fear that Mother and the rest of my family might still be under all the debris, so I hastily said good-bye before the tears came.

It seemed that the best place to resume my search was the Red Cross center. So I walked back and reported for duty. Every supply truck took the names of my family to the next Red Cross center where they would make deliveries. Two days, and still no news. Many new names were added to the "found" list but not those of my family. Worry occupied every waking moment, and most sleeping ones.

The third day, when I was in the middle of serving the soup, one of our delivery men came straight to me, his face radiating good news. "I think I have found your family," he said. I started crying. Putting his arms around me, he told of the remote farm house where a family of five was looking for their oldest daughter. "Don't stand there crying. I will take you there so you can check the story out."

For an hour we hobbled over the most deserted country path. Suddenly, there they were. They had heard us coming from afar—Mother, and Nellie, Tine, Johanna, and Kobie. We all laughed and cried at the same time. After a while we sat down right then and there and talked. Mother said, "At the first sound of the air raid alarm I gathered the kids and ran home, hoping you would do the same. But just around the corner the bombs began to fall. So we raced to the air raid shelter. There was no more room, so we ran to the next one near our house even while the bombing was going on. It too was full, even more than usual. Suddenly, the ground where we stood started shaking, so we plunged into the already full shelter on top of others. Kobie and I could have been crushed to death. When we heard the planes leave, we stumbled out of the shelter, blinking in the sunlight. I could not believe the number of screaming and yelling people.

"Then, as the thick dust clouds began to rise, I saw that our house was no more; the whole street was aflame. We ran—we never stopped running until we came upon a farmer's horsedrawn wagon. The farmer invited as many people as the wagon could hold to get in and escape the devastation. He brought us here to his lovely farm. He even promised to go to town in a few days and check out where you were, but he was apparently in no hurry. And now, Nettie, you have found us instead." How we praised God together that no one in our closest family was even hurt. We were delighted to have found each other.

Mother was bravely accepting the fact that every possession was lost. The full impact of our material loss was felt later. Furniture could be replaced, but photographs and family heirlooms, jewelry, and other sentimental items could not. But we were not concerned about that just then. Living quarters had to be found and immediate needs taken care of.

With relief, I returned to my volunteer duties. Back at the Red Cross center, I was put right to work. Trucks were arriving from all over the Netherlands. Churches and other organizations had sent clothing, all lovingly washed and ironed, ready for immediate use. The clothing had to be unpacked, hung on hangers, and sorted according to sizes. Arranging shoes, socks, underwear, dresses, shirts, and all the other items kept us busy for the next couple of days.

In the midst of all this activity came the message that every homeless child less than fourteen could be registered and given temporary homes with church members throughout the Netherlands. Since Mother had four eligible children, I went to talk this possibility over with her. Though reluctant, she was willing to let my four sisters be registered, perhaps giving *her* a better chance to find emergency housing. The decision to part was met with mixed feelings of joy and sadness. Where would my sisters be placed? Would they be treated right? Would they become homesick? Would we be able to visit them? Would we ever be together again, all of us?

Parting became a little easier when we knew where they would be going. Most churches were involved in providing temporary homes; we told the kids that they were going on vacation to visit lovely Christian families. Nellie and Tine would go to Nyverdal on the German border. Johanna was assigned to a family in Utrecht, a big city about fifty miles from our city. Our little sister Kobie would go to Goudriaan, a farming community in the southern part of Holland. Finally the day arrived for their departure. The buses were slowly loaded. It was heartbreaking to say good-bye. The children pressed their noses, wet from crying, against the windows. Many pleaded to stay. But at last every detail was worked out. Slowly the buses started moving away, with parents running beside them to throw kisses and to give encouraging words to their crying young ones. With the buses gone, the parents did not have to appear brave anymore. Everyone cried freely.

I am sure I will never comprehend what must have gone on in Mother's mind. She betrayed no emotion; her face was stony. Was that a weapon to prevent her mind from snapping? Did she shed all her tears in secret? Why could she not share her sorrow with me, and let me share mine with her? I felt so incapable of helping her. Why didn't she cry?

Together we turned away quietly. Each of us was involved in her own thoughts. We could *feel* the emptiness of the adults, suddenly deprived of the happy chatter of kids around them. I went with Mother back to the farmhouse to pick up her meager belongings and say, "Thank you," to the kind farmer's family. We would have to search for a place for Mother to stay. The Red Cross center had a street map from which we could determine which homes had escaped the devastating fires. One of those was the house of a very well-to-do uncle on Mother's side, so we made plans to go there. After a long walk to the farmhouse, Mother said, "I'd like to say good-bye to these people myself; maybe you can gather my things over there in the corner of the barn."

At this chance to be alone for a moment, I sat in that corner and bawled. I thought of my departed sisters, and even cried at the sight of Mother's belongings. They consisted of four army blankets, several ugly towels, a meager set of clothing, and a toothbrush. I knew that if I did not get hold of myself quickly, I would go crazy, so again I quoted Scripture:

All Thy breakers and Thy waves have rolled over me.
The Lord will command His lovingkindness in the daytime;
And His song will be with me in the night. . . .
Hope in God, for I shall yet praise Him.

Psalm 42:7-8, 11

Again restored in my faith, I was assured that my Lord would not leave me, nor ever forsake me (Hebrews 13:5).

Finally, Mother emerged from the farmhouse with the farmer's wife. I shook hands with the woman and wholeheartedly thanked her for the care of our family. With renewed determination, we headed toward the Hoflaan where Uncle lived. Oom Jan (Uncle John), eighty years old, lived with his wife, Heintje, and their unmarried daughter in an expensive home. However, the German occupation forces had knocked on their door one day and, after examining the roomy house, forced them to share it with a big family.

These strangers had probably pledged allegiance to Hitler's philosophy, for only such people were placed in such beautiful homes. It was unusual practice that our relatives were allowed to stay. One word of complaint from the "live-in" family to the authorities, and my uncle and aunt would be thrown out into the streets, no matter how old they were. Every home that still stood was visited by the occupation authorities, with the usual result that extra families were to be situated there. Sometimes even two or three families were added.

But Mother and I did not know that on the day we rang their doorbell. Uncle opened the door and peered over his glasses. A bright smile of recognition came over his always jolly face. I could still remember how, when we were children, he would cut out of newspapers a whole set of boys and girls holding hands. At other times, by folding paper a certain way, we would make a boat that could float. Seeing someone so dear brightened my spirits.

After the happy greetings were over and tea was made, Uncle said to Mother, "Teuntje, tell me now what happened with you and your children. Are they all alive and well?" For several hours we shared our past experiences.

When all was told, Uncle John scratched his head and told us in whispers about the family living with them—with all those wild kids running around their priceless furniture. "If you can put up with that, Teuntje," Uncle said, "you are more than welcome to sleep on our couch." They were so gracious and kind and willing to help. They would have been happy to squeeze me in somewhere too, but I did not want to be confined in such a crowded situation. Besides, I was confident that Mother would be well cared for.

Uncle, who was well-to-do, owned a large part of the Northern Island. It lay in the heavily bombed part of the harbor between the two bridges that separated the southern suburbs of Rotterdam from the other part. If any of Uncle's property on the Northern Island remained and could be made livable, Mother would be given first choice. Because this was not immediately clear, she was welcome to stay with them in the meantime. Mother was reluctant for me to go away again. She knew, however, that I would feel like a bird in a cage. I was still the child of the wide-open spaces, and so she agreed to let me go check if any of my friends from the Salvation

Army were alive, and whether they would have room for me. Perhaps, if their homes had escaped the raging fires, I could stay a week or two with them until the future looked more certain. Somehow, I was convinced that this wretched war would soon be over. Maybe I could help at the Red Cross center until then.

Mother and I had been able to communicate much better since the family had been reunited. She talked freely about her escape and how glad she had been that none of us was hurt. I in turn spoke of my experiences, particularly when there was no path out of the fires. Maybe it was because none of my sisters was there to interrupt, but Mother and I were finally able to talk naturally with each other. I admired her courage, for she had endured much. First the tragic losses of Maria and my twin Frankie, then her husband; and now all her earthly possessions were gone. She had nothing left even to lay her head on, only a borrowed couch. Sending her children into homes scattered throughout the country must have added to her sorrow. I saw this brave woman, my mother, in a different light.

These were only a few of the many heartaches around us to deal with. There were no answers, no solutions that we could see. We could only pray. Prayer for my relationship with Mother was now being answered. We were both expressing more understanding for each other and there was more warmth between us. When I left the house in Kralingen, we parted as friends and promised to keep in close touch. The foremost thing in our minds was to survive both mentally and physically to the best of our ability.

When the door shut behind me, I walked slowly back to the Red Cross center. Tomorrow I would officially quit, I decided. At the shelter there were hundreds of people without a place to go. I was given a cot to sleep on, like all the other Red Cross workers. I was in dreadful need of a bath and a shampoo; it had been more than a week since my last one. I needed some other clothes, too. In my concern to find my family, I had not bothered about my own needs. I still wore the clothing that I had on the day of the fire. With the worry about my family taken care of, I suddenly felt overwhelmed by loneliness. It was my turn to dish out the evening meal, but I was in no shape to be serving others. I was drained! I lay down on my cot, sobbing, and unburdened the load to my Lord. I was so unbelievably tired that I could not do anything else but just lie there and begin to feel sorry for myself. I knew that it was a dangerous state to be in. Wallowing in self-pity is never the answer, but I felt so helpless and could not see one step in front of me.

Slowly, like a soft spring rain, came the blessing spoken so many times at the closing of a church service.

> The peace of God, which surpasses all comprehension, shall guard your hearts and your minds in Christ Jesus.

What I had heard so many times from Philippians 4:7 was now the answer God was giving me—I *would* survive, both mentally and physically! I had that promise from the Creator of the universe. Again I saw the golden thread of God's care weaving itself through my life. I was so aware of His presence. In that stillness and peace, I laid every problem before Him. Confident that Jesus could supply all my needs, I fell asleep peacefully secured in His love.

I awoke the following morning with new hope. But it was not long before I saw new problems developing. We had been wondering why those trucks, which had brought emergency aid from many parts of our country, had not been sent back. We also questioned the special attention the Nazis showed in caring for those trucks. We even began to think that maybe the Nazis were not as bad as we had been made to believe they were. But it wasn't long until we changed our thinking. That morning, two big trucks loaded with German soldiers arrived. We could not understand their language, but their loud shouting and fist-waving promised us something was going to happen.

Two by two, holding loaded guns, they went to each farmhouse. All the farmers in the area were forced to drive their cattle and hogs to designated central points and load them into the waiting trucks to be taken to Germany. The cattle and hogs were the farmer's livelihood. Naturally they would protest this order. When they did, however, guns were shoved between their ribs. Farmers who had no livestock were ordered to drive their plows onto the trucks. Everything was in chaos. The noise of the animals crammed into the trucks could be heard everywhere. The streets were full of plows, tractors, and other farm implements waiting to be loaded. Frightened women and children were sent home while the men worked late into the night. The whole convoy was to be loaded and ready to leave at daybreak. Nazis with rifles were stationed as watchmen, so that nothing would delay the departure of the trucks. After all the vehicles were loaded, the men returned to their farms.

Nobody slept much that night. Suddenly, we were all aroused by shouting and screaming. Everyone was ordered to come to the central gathering-place across from the convoy. We noticed something strange about the trucks loaded with our animals and farm machinery; they looked crooked. When we dared to look a little closer, we saw that every tire had been slashed. It had happened unnoticed by the guards. Probably the animals had made enough noise to "screen" this daring, successful act. Nobody knew for sure who had done it, but it had to be the men from our area. Any feelings of gratified amusement were soon turned into fear because of what we now could barely see through the mist of the early dawn. Out of the farmhouses came the fathers of families with small children. The men were being driven out by Nazi soldiers. With their hands over their heads and guns in their backs, they too were brought to the central gathering-point. We heard an Army truck approaching. Every uniformed Nazi jumped to attention. Out leaped an officer of the Gestapo, the most feared Nazis of all. He shouted commands and then went into the crowd, choosing at random several teenaged boys. They were loaded into the Army truck and driven away. They were never seen again.

With the Gestapo gone, the Nazi soldiers forced our men to unload the animals and the farm equipment and repair the tires. After the job was completed, the trucks had to be reloaded. How they crammed all those animals and equipment into those trucks was beyond our knowledge. If it was meant to put fear into our hearts, the Nazis certainly succeeded. What they did not know was that a desire for revenge was also born that night. Several days later the convoy finally left. We were relieved to see it go, regardless of the fact that what it carried belonged to us. In the next five years, scenes like this happened over and over until the Nazis had plundered every area of Holland, Belgium, and France, as well as other European countries.

One day I overheard someone ask one of the Nazi soldiers, "When are you planning to leave?"

The soldier answered, "We are not leaving till every Dutchman eats grass."

Now I felt even more strongly that I wanted to get away. Soon afterward the Red Cross center was closed, and I began searching for my friends.

11

Jake

While I was looking for my Christian friends, I unexpectedly found a Salvation Army member I knew. I had felt so lonely, and now, here was Lientje. Only a few months earlier, her mother had died. She and her father had begun helping others to get over their own heartache. How nice it was when she asked me to go home with her. When Lientje's dad saw us coming, he stretched out both his hands and gave me a warm welcome. Lientje made a pot of tea while we all relaxed, and they asked about my experiences. As they listened, tears formed in their eyes.

Their house had been spared, but not by much. Their front window looked out over the scarred city. When they heard of my need for temporary shelter, they offered to let me stay with them. How wonderful this was! Finally, I could bathe and wash my hair. That was another answered prayer. They themselves were sorrowing over the recent death of their loved one, yet they made room for me in their hearts and in their home. My prayers to be with God's people were answered. The Bible says, "I will instruct you and teach you in the way which you should go; I will counsel you with My eye upon you" (Psalm 32:8).

That evening, every member of our Salvation

Army corps that they had been able to locate came to welcome me. How precious is the fellowship of believers! Many stories were exchanged, and much praise was given to our wonderful Lord. It was an extra treat to see my *special* friend, Jake, the handsome young man who now wore the Salvation Army uniform. It seemed a lifetime since we had seen each other. We had so much to talk about.

After the evening was over and the others prepared to go, he said, "Nettie, do you feel like taking a walk?"

"Sure," I said, "we have a lot of catching up to do. I will be right with you." In another room, I took a hasty look in the mirror, congratulating myself on my shining clean and set hairdo. I then put on the only sweater I owned and I was ready for my walk with Jake. By the light of a dim moon, I saw how tall and handsome Jake was. For hours we walked. At first I was quite surprised to feel his strong arm around me—shyly he had explained that this was to prevent me from falling over the debris still quite evident everywhere. A second surprise was that uncharacteristically, I became the listener and he the talker. Walking slowly away from the city, we soon found ourselves by Father's lake.

I heard Jake's voice asking me, "Where have you been? I went half-crazy on the other side of Rotterdam's bridges. The first day I had seen hundreds of parachutes open with men and equipment and yes, even jeeps falling out of one of the many German airplanes. They just kept coming. Then I saw the repeated bombing of the airport and all the oil tanks from Shell on fire. What a nightmare!" I did not say anything in response to Jake; I only made sounds of agreement. Despite the horror in his words, his voice was like music to me.

He continued, "Were you not terribly frightened that morning, Nettie? I went to the bridges to come over to your side, but everywhere I heard explosions and shooting and also saw many groups of Nazi soldiers. There was no way to get to you."

"Then on Tuesday, I saw the city burn. I remember the date clearly: May 14th, 1940. I remember it, Nettie, because I never thought to see you anymore!" I was so surprised to hear him speak like that. Nobody ever seemed worried about me, yet here was a young man who said he could not sleep for worry about me. I was speechless from happiness, drinking up all his caring words.

"Nettie," he said, "I prayed night and day for you, so we would meet again! And here you are! Do you know I have become an official soldier in the Salvation Army? I look real good in my uniform, and I play a trombone now; I am glad the bandmaster thought I had enough theory lessons in music!"

Without noticing, we had arrived again in front of Lientje's house, I felt kind of sorry about that, but Jake, shy again, suddenly asked if he could pick me up even a little early the following night. More eagerly than I anticipated, I said, "Sure, I will be ready at seven!"

Singing gaily, I went upstairs where I found Lientje still waiting. Her father had retired earlier. She was a pleasant, quiet girl with the voice of an angel; she had often sung solo for us. Now, after my walk with Jake, her bright eyes shared her eager curiosity, awaiting what I would tell her.

"Oh, Lientje, he is nice! Can you imagine that he was so worried about me? To my shame, I have to confess I thought about all of you in the back of my mind, but I never particularly singled one person out."

"Well, Nettie," she said, "he cares a great deal about you. Dad and I both think that he is in love with you." Again I was surprised. I had just come through a series of difficult months. First my conversion, then my change of life-style, then a horrifying experience in almost losing my life. It seemed so unbelievable that someone who could choose any available girl would choose the one who least expected it. It made me so happy. "Well," Lientje yawned, "Happy dreams. I have to go to work tomorrow; you can sit here, but I'm going to sleep."

The following day, Lientje's father made me sit down while he made breakfast for me. This was an added blessing, for I had begun to feel just how exhausted I was. That morning, I had slept almost to ten o'clock, which was very unusual. Everything seemed to tire me unbelievably. I felt I should have gone to see Mother, but I just had to sleep and when later in the morning I was alone, I went back to bed again. Everybody was so kind here, and I drank it in. That evening at seven on the dot, the doorbell rang, and there was Jake. He did not want to come in. "Nettie," he said, "my mother wants to see you! I have told her that I found you again; is that all right with you?"

"Sure, I'd love to go; I hope she will like me?"

Laughingly, Jake teased me for being afraid. I was indeed a little apprehensive so soon after meeting Jake. Because it was at least an hour's walk, we stepped along faster than I would have liked to. Along the way my personal happiness was temporarily set aside when I saw the full extent of the war's devastation. The bombing had almost completely destroyed the Doostplein Plaza once surrounded by hundreds of homes. Now only the mill was standing, its blades straight up in the center. It is an old custom for millers to express their state of mind by the position of the wings of their mills, when these are still. The big mill in the center of the city which miraculously escaped the fire had its wings in a mourning position. The Hoogstreet, the Goudsesinged, the beautiful Maasstation where once trains served all of Europe—all of these famous landmarks were completely in ruins. Big steel beams stuck at crazy angles in the air. Debris was so *thick!*

"Jake where are they going to put all that rubble?"

"Well," said Jake, "I'll show you." He took me through some side streets to the site where one of our most beautiful canals had once been located. Where gracious white swans had once been fed on Sunday afternoons and where people had gaily skated in winter, now they were filling it up with the rubble. They were making streets from our once proud waterways.

It was good to feel Jake's arm supporting me, for I felt faint. "Let's go," I said, "I have seen enough!" We got to Jake's house a little late. I was glad his mother was alone. Seeing my white tear-stained face and my red nose, Jake told his mother that I had just seen the damage in the city and that I was upset about it.

Jake's lovely mother said, "Just trust in God. He is in control. Soon He will return, and He wants us all to be faithful until that day."

When I had had a cup of tea, I said, "Could you tell me what I should do first? I don't even have any papers that officially tell who I am. Nor does Mother."

"Yes," she said, "Nearby there is a set of newly-erected wooden buildings where you can register; there you will receive a gray card with your identification stamped on it. That will give you access to food rations and also help you obtain assistance in relocation. Your mother can also get help in obtaining the most needed supplies. Churches all over the rest of Holland have sent truckloads of furniture, clothing, pots and pans, and anything else useful to help people who lost everything. And I will myself gather what our families can help you with.

"At those same wooden buildings, you and your mother can each get a ration of stamps to set up housekeeping. You better do all that right away tomorrow; you are already late!" What a marvelous woman Jake's mother was!

After a hug, she waved goodbye from her window until we turned the corner. I felt so much better. It was late when Jake dropped me off at home. He didn't stay, for he still had to walk for the fourth time the hour back to his own home.

That was the beginning of a friendship that turned into love. One evening he took me just over the bridge by the canal and asked, "Nettie, would you marry me?"

I did not hesitate for one minute. Jake had impressed me first of all with his solid belief in Jesus Christ as his Savior, with sound character, *and* with his love for me. Looking into his blue eyes, I solemnly answered, "Yes, Jake, I love you!"

It was a simple silver ring he slid onto my finger—no diamonds and no gold, for it was wartime—but I never saw one more beautiful to me. I knew that I could trust him and count on his solid strength. We returned to tell our friends we were engaged. How different ugly circumstances can appear when you are in love! Suddenly all my hardships were being shared by someone else who cared for me. Jake and I were able to laugh together and work together, and above all else, to pray together.

Soon another very important event took place. Our two Salvation Army officers had asked advice from headquarters in Amsterdam about the problem of being without a real meeting-place. Our building had been destroyed.

The unusual answer to the problem brought a lot of fanfare into Rotterdam. The city officials were notified, as was the press. The Salvation Army band rehearsed. The songleader prepared special music for his choir. Every uniform was pressed for the "arrival" of our new meeting-place. We were all so jubilant! All were standing in great expectation for "its" arrival at the *canal,* for it was a boat! It seemed that all of Holland had come to celebrate with us. There it was; we could see the familiar yellow, red, and blue Salvation Army flag flying in the breeze high on the mast. We would be worshiping on a former hospital ship donated by the Red Cross.

The ship tied up at the dock, near the very spot where Jake and I stood, and we could clearly see the Salvation Army symbols already painted across its side. The staunch Dutch were never given to showing much emotion, but on this occasion, there were few dry eyes. While policemen kept the crowd at a safe distance, the gangplank was secured and the band played. There was loud applause. There had been very little to applaud in recent days. After the ribbon-cutting ceremony, a small group of us entered the ship to begin scrubbing and polishing our "Ark." We had only a few days to make it presentable for Sunday service.

We started out checking what we had to do. Luckily everything was already painted in light gray oil base paint. But it all was filthy. There were plenty of benches without backs, which would be tiresome to sit on for extended periods of time, especially for the elderly. But that was not our concern yet. Jake, Henk, and Koos began stacking all the benches in the back of the room. The happy talking and shouting made this work fun. But it didn't go that quickly. Rina, Cor, Dini, and I were chasing each other over and around the dirty benches, teasing the boys out of their wits. But the fellows soon retaliated. They quietly whispered to each other; next time Rina and Dini jumped on a bench, the boys lifted it way up in the air, quite naturally causing further screams: "Hey you guys, let me down; I'll fall," and on it went until finally we decided seriously to start working.

We had bought a big dish of oil soap. Everyone had brought rags and pails and scrub brushes. And how we worked. The men washed the ceilings and the women washed the seemingly endless long walls. The floor had not seen water for a decade, we were sure. It all went so slowly. That night we went for more helpers; several older men and women came to help the following day. Finally, four days later on a Saturday morning, that boat smelled as clean as it looked.

We were all inspecting and checking the last details when Jake said, "I am going home. I'm tired; I'll see you tomorrow." One after the other left. Wearily, as I too left, I stopped across the street to look back. There I saw the Salvation Army flag blowing in the wind. And a warm feeling took hold of me, for that flag stood for all we believed in. Its main color was red—that color stood for the cleansing blood of Jesus Christ, who died for me and indeed, all of us in Rotterdam. He brought hope to a lost world. Today there is a song sung by the new generation of Salvation Army people. It would have been appropriate then:

The hoodlum, the hooker, and the hobo,
Are gonna feel at home in heaven
(Because of that Blood).
The drug addict and the drunkard
And the dropouts are gonna get their sins forgiven
(Because of that Blood).
The man who knows his need and will admit it
Will find God as a remedy to fit it
(Because of that Blood).
The hoodlum, the hooker and hobo
Are gonna walk the streets of gold
(Because of the Blood).
Yes, the hoodlum, the hooker, and hobo
Will walk the streets of God
(Because of that Blood).*

It was as William Booth, the founder of the Salvation Army, said. He gave this command to his soldiers: "Go for the souls and go for the worst." I looked again at the Salvation Army flag. The border was blue, to represent the purity of God. The yellow star in the center was the symbol of the Holy Spirit. In our own harbor city, I was proud to be part of God's command to go out and preach the gospel. We all went back to our own places, knowing that tomorrow our ark would be filled with needy people.

On Sunday the boat was filled, though it could hold only about one hundred and fifty people. The hard benches were uncomfortable, but that did not dampen the joyful spirit of our praise and thanksgiving service. Everyone was quiet and attentive as the guest speaker from Amsterdam headquarters opened his Bible to Acts 27:2 and read about how the apostles found a ship and went aboard. He

---

*From the Salvation Army musical, "The Blood of the Lamb," by Lt.-Colonel John Gowans and Lt.-Colonel John Larsson.

spoke of Paul's journey and the safe landing after the great storm. The impressive service marked a glad new beginning.

We held services in our ark for just a half year. One day in the spring of 1941, my boss called me into the office where I also found Jake. He said wearily, "You two can take the rest of the day off."

Jake seemed very disturbed, and immediately I thought, "They must have called him into the service." But when I asked him, he only shook his head. I thought he was going to cry. What could it be? I hurried to get my coat and the minute we were out the door I asked, "What happened?"

With tears in his eyes Jake said, "Nettie, they have forbidden the Salvation Army to function. Our ark has been confiscated by the Germans. They have already painted over the name, our flag is gone, and the officers are gone. Vanished! We don't know if they've been sent away or what."

"But why?" I asked, stunned by the news. "The Salvation Army is *helping* everywhere; why can't we be what we want? We're no danger to the Nazis." We were both sick at heart.

Finally Jake said, "Nettie, I don't know why, but let's go and see what we can find out for ourselves."

In silence and with heavy steps, we arrived at the docks; we could hardly believe what they'd done to our beautiful ark. With green army paint, they had painted over the sides where we so proudly had displayed our Salvation Army name. The bridge of the ship was locked, and there was a notice posted which read: "It is forbidden by order of Seyss-Inquart [the Reich Commissioner appointed by the Führer] to use this boat for any public gatherings. Anyone disobeying this order is subject to extreme punishment."

Sadly, we went straight to Lientje's house. Harry was there, too. They were reading a small newspaper that included this notice.

> As an Organization controlled by England, the Salvation Army has ceased to exist. Any person wearing the former uniform will be punished. Any home or meetingplace where more than seven persons are gathered will be subject to immediate search with the occupants subject to be sent to Germany to help in the war effort.
>
> Seyss Inquart,
> Reich Commissioner

In the next days we prayed and prayed and asked our heavenly Father for guidance. We visited every person who was in one way or another attached to our service. On Sunday, we were all assigned to a certain home, with each of us choosing a different time of arrival, for safety's sake. We started with a prayer meeting. Oh, how we prayed! We expected at any minute to hear the Nazis pounding on our door. But how precious is the fellowship of the saints! We dared not sing hymns, so we read them out loud. Then one of us would tell about the care God had given His children. One after another said, "I lost my home, but I still have Jesus. He is my strength every day." We prayed for every officer we knew, wondering all the while about their whereabouts. We prayed for our Queen Wilhelmina in England, for our Crown Princess Juliana in Ottawa, Canada. Then we held hands and prayed God's blessing upon each one of us. One by one we left at staggered intervals.

We became very clever at hiding our meeting times. A child at the window was assigned to watch for danger. The testimonies in those services were heartwarming, and reminded us of similar situations in the early church as documented in the book of Acts.

One day, we had a visit from a new officer. She was wearing her navy blue uniform but without any of the usual markings. She had official papers with her and asked us to call a meeting. Each of us in the "inner core" of our organization gathered at one of the bigger homes. There she spoke, "Until the war is ended and while we are under German occupation, we cannot be called the Salvation Army any more. But we *are* allowed to be a mission group. We can wear our uniforms without any outside signs, without the Salvation "S" and without rank. We are also forbidden to wear our regular headdress. Just put them carefully away; save them for the day when the war's over. Please keep yourself strictly to these orders, so we can at least have our open meetings back. Remember that the Salvation Army flag cannot be displayed either, but keep it close by for the day when we will all celebrate our freedom and we can proudly raise it on high!" We served under her until the end of the war. Our services were held in a hastily erected, often drafty wooden barrack. At least we had a place where we could freely worship.

12

Narrow Escapes

Rotterdam's streets were covered with at least three feet of debris from the bombing. This was a hindrance to the Nazis. At first they hired men to clear those highways. This vast undertaking took months. As soon as one area was cleared, wooden barracks were built for the thousands of homeless families who now occupied buildings more useful to the Germans. Also, rows of barracks were raised for the bakers and the grocers who had to fill the needs of the population. Jake worked in such a place for a while. One day he overslept and was an hour and a half late to work. While he was gone, the Nazis, not satisfied with their quota of men for Germany, had come and taken at gunpoint every man there. They were loaded onto huge trucks and, without even being allowed to say good-bye to their families, they were transported to Germany. Jake had missed it all because he overslept. God heard the prayer of a mother. The golden thread of His care again came through.

After that incident, the other men kept Jake a little in the background. For a couple of months everything went well. Other young men, tired of hiding and in dire financial need, came to take the place of the men who had been taken. One day the Nazis again came to fill their quota, but Jake was home in bed with high fever and tonsilitis. He had escaped again! But after that, it became too dangerous to return to work. The Nazis' returns were more and more frequent, because they needed more and more men to fight their war. So Jake chose again to hide "permanently."

While all of this had been happening, my mother's uncle had secured the City Hall's permission for her move into one of his houses on the Northern Island. On the island between the two bridges where the war had been fought in the first days, nothing had escaped extreme damage. Mother and I and Uncle John had gone together to inspect the new apartment. It was in terrible shape. The bullets had gone in through the front and out through the back. Uncle sent some men right off to fix the holes. Wallpaper was added and the woodwork was painted. Mother and I scrubbed away all the dirt. As soon as possible, we wanted my sisters back home; we wanted to be a family again.

So the following day we went to the Dutch Red Cross post where war victims could share goods gathered from cities all over Holland—cities that had escaped the physical devastation that Rotterdam had experienced. We were given a card and number that meant we were a family with young children and with no head of the house to provide for them. Still, we could choose just so much, for there were many equally needy. We got two double beds with bedding and blankets for six people, two wooden straight chairs, and a small table. Then a big and a small pan to cook in, a hot plate to cook on, six plates, and silverware. We also received some coupons we could buy smaller items with. We were so thankful, first of all, for an apartment all our own. Twenty-six thousand people had lost their homes, and everyone was fighting for living space. Our living space was on the second floor above a butcher shop located on an island in Rotterdam's harbor, and now Mother began planning to bring my sisters back "home."

Mother had also become a faithful member of a small church; the congregation was certainly following the teachings of the Bible in pouring out love and kindness to a widow. They helped Mother establish her new home and supplied some of the basic items she did not have.

We also learned a valuable lesson that many are unwilling to learn—that it is not only blessed to give but also gracious to receive. We still had a lot of pride, but it is one of those seven sins that God despises, and Mother and I were learning that lesson. Some of these willing people were not always tactful in their giving. It bothered Mother and me when we invited people for tea and they showed up with chairs that needed much repair, pots and pans banged up and without covers, or worn-out clothes for us. We had to understand that our affluent times were over and these were the only things available, for we were not the only ones in need. Many times we had to swallow our pride.

We furnished the house as fast as we could so we could bring my sisters back home. Soon we were able to do just that, after long separation. First Nellie and Tine came back home. They looked so healthy. They came by train and were dressed from top to bottom. In a big suitcase there were handmade sweaters, socks, and plenty of dresses. Everyone in the city of Nyverdal seemed to have outdone themselves in their giving, to make up for the hardship my sisters had gone through. A few days later our Johanna came home, also with a loaded suitcase and with stories and more stories. We were all at home when our little sister Kobie came back from the farm community where she had been sent. The couple she had been with also brought cheese and meat and ham; we never felt so rich. When we were finally together we prayed and thanked God for seeing us through in such tragic times. What happy times for Mother!

We soon realized that our location in the center of the harbor became a real disadvantage. For the next five years of war, we lived with daily bombing. The island was a strategic area, extremely valuable to both the Allies and the Nazis. And their bombs did not distinguish friend from foe. This constant apprehension, plus having only two beds for six people, made me realize I had to get a place of my own. I again began to feel closed-in since the return of my sisters. Mother never told me I had to leave, but the situation was impossible for me, and I'm sure she knew it. I also needed a job.

In seeking employment, my experience at the Red Cross and the things I had learned in the five years working at the Van Es home seemed to point to training as a practical nurse. Mother seemed happy with the idea, considering it a respectful occupation for me at least, so I agreed to the job. The hospital where I studied supplied us trainees with desperately needed room and board. So at least I had my own bed to sleep in. Mother, who felt badly to see me go, sewed all the required uniforms for me. Somehow I knew she was proud of me.

Because of all the suffering at the hospital, I soon was very much aware that nursing was not my life's calling. I had too soft a heart for it; when someone died, I died. And many died, because this was a place only for the severely ill. For many whose wounds or illnesses would have been severe enough for hospitalization in peacetime, there was no room, and they were turned away at the hospital door. When someone was hurting, I felt their pain. I knew I had to keep trying, but it was a nightmare for me, particularly because I also lived there. There seemed no escape from the pathos, the suffering. So one day, much to the dismay of Mother (who never could understand why that nurse's uniform didn't do anything for me) I asked to be hired in the kitchen instead, trading my uniform for an apron.

Mother again became disappointed in me. "How could you *do* that Nettie? A nurse is important and respected. Any Dutch woman can be a cook. Where's the future in that?"

But I could only answer, "The most important thing to me is to keep my sanity." She did not, *could* not understand.

Another concern was my fiancé, Jake. The fact that he could at any moment be inducted into the Führer's army was my daily fear. He had been working in his brother-in-law's bakery, fifteen miles away. He rode all that distance back and forth daily on his bicycle, for jobs were hard to come by. I am sure that only the faithful prayers of his godly mother, as well as my own, kept him from being caught and inducted. The Germans were suffering massive losses on the Russian front. Hitler's need for men to fight his war soon resulted in what were called *razzia.* Men were snatched right off the street, or homes were raided by the ever-feared Gestapo. With loaded guns, Nazis rampaged through our streets and homes, not content until they filled their quota. Many fathers and sons were abducted and taken away without even an opportunity to notify their families.

Most Dutch families organized a warning system. In the evening the families in each row of houses would gather together for economic reasons. We had already been deprived of municipal electricity for a long time. Every window was covered with the required black window shade so no light could be seen from the outside, not even candlelight. We knew that even the faintest light could be seen from the air. And we knew how the Nazis would quickly come down on a "careless household." In most homes two heavy-duty hooks screwed into the ceiling beams held chains fastened to a bicycle dangling in the air. Each person had to take his turn peddling for fifteen minutes so the generator could provide power for the bike's headlight to illuminate the room. This provided light to work puzzles, play board games, or read.

A coded doorbell ring was devised. If the doorbell suddenly rang, but not in the prearranged code, it could be the Gestapo conscripting men. While the young and sometimes not-so-young men raced for their hiding places, all traces of their ever having been there had to be erased as quickly as possible. Many people owned a furiously barking dog that had to be tied up "before the door could be opened," thus extending the time for the men to hide.

Our neighbor, for instance, once showed me a point of their carpet that covered a trap door leading to a closet in the apartment below. That closet looked like a corner in the downstairs living room. It was covered with wallpaper that matched the rest of the room. In this small square closet, the men would hide and wait and pray. Those prayers sustained the woman who had to open the door to the Nazis. Her face could not reveal fear or apprehension. While the men were hiding, the children were trained to sip Father's coffee, and the fourteen-year-old son would hold the pipe the oldest brother had been smoking. All this had to take place in a few seconds, including tying up the barking dog. The Gestapo would not hesitate to kick down the door. Everyone would have to look as surprised as possible as the Nazis banged on walls, opened closets, and looked under beds. The mother would stand there expressionless and *pray!*

As fast as those intruders came in, they left again, but often they would stop in their tracks abruptly to look back into the face of a child. They hoped that the child might give an involuntary glance at the place where a father or brother was hidden. We would wait until we heard them marching off. Our hearts were often saddened, because we knew the sounds of the uneven footsteps were those of men who had been found in their hiding places in other neighborhood apartments. At least we could turn back the carpet corner and open the trap door of the hidden closet to let our own men out. With faces as white as sheets, they would bow their heads in thankful prayer to God. A person learned fast in such dark days to rely on God.

There might even be a relatively quiet time for a month or two, and so the young fellows were not so careful anymore. They even ventured out for fresh air and visited nearby friends and relatives. While the men were out, they were often surprised by an army truck driving at high speed and filled with Nazis who jumped off and grabbed any man in sight. Families and loved ones were left destitute without any income, as the men were shipped immediately to Germany.

Because our country had been plundered of all

bare essentials, central kitchens were set up to supply each ration card holder with a small daily bowl of tulip-bulb soup. This gray mush was swallowed quickly and never tasted—never allowed to linger on the tongue—but it kept us alive.

Jake could no longer work for his brother-in-law at the distant bakery. He also had to go into hiding. One day he would be in his mother's house; on other days, he would stay with a married sister or brother. He had to hide in many different places so that he would not bring danger to his family. We saw each other for very short periods; they were becoming less frequent, but more precious, too. Living at opposite ends of town made it ever more difficult for us to be together. After being shifted from one address to another, one of the relatives in sympathy with our predicament offered to rent us an attic room so that we could get married. We had already been waiting for four years for the war to end.

We went to ask advice of our Salvation Army officer. She warned us of the hardship we would have to endure as a married couple. "You'll never know if Jake will ever return when he leaves you, Nettie. Jake, you'll never know that Nettie—or even the apartment—will still be there when you return. You will see hunger in each other's eyes, and it will touch you even more deeply than in strangers. Your fears will all be doubled, because they will now apply to you *both.* And yet, all these things are bearable to lovers who also love God. For His love will find you in all this rubble and feed your hunger with His promise of everlasting peace."

We couldn't believe that anything could be any worse than it already was. So we decided that we would get married and rent the attic room.

13

Together in the Attic

We had a very small wedding with a short ceremony by the Salvation Army officer and only a few
of our closest relatives and friends present. However,
as we applied for a marriage license at the city hall,
we were not aware that these records were checked
by the Nazis. Promptly our ration card was held
back. We were now on the Gestapo's most-wanted
list, earmarked for special attention. At the most unexpected times, night or day, they came to search for
Jake. Our situation became desperate. It was not
safe for us that too many people knew Jake was still
around and in hiding. So as quietly as possible, we
moved as a married couple into the upstairs apartment with only one small window in the slanted
roof. All we could see was sky. There we spent all of
the daytime; only occasionally at night would we
dare to visit our relatives or friends. We kept occupied by playing games or by reading, always ready
on the spur of the moment to wipe out any sign of
existence. It had to appear that the room was only a
spare bedroom. We became experts in this game of
staying alive.

On the other side of the two bridges where our
new attic apartment was, lived a Salvation Army
captain and his wife, Betty. They were a wonderful
godly couple. Being a member of the clergy with the

right "credentials," the captain could travel freely. He had connections everywhere and could supply occasional rations from underground sources. We became fast friends. That couple had a complete system set up to help others.

How fervently that man could pray, pleading with God for help! He brought potatoes to us when there were none to be bought with *gold*. His lovely wife made "miracle" soup from what seemed no more than water for ingredients. This soup kept many people alive in hiding. Captain could also make you laugh until your belly hurt from something other than hunger. For instance, once I left our closet door open and he saw several of my hats (one with a very long feather) and a shawl or two. While we were busy talking, he planted that feathery hat on his head and wound a shawl around his neck and asked in a strained high voice if anyone wanted to go for a walk with him. Silly? Of course. But we roared with laughter. Again, he had kept us from going out of our minds. He was always optimistic, always encouraging, and always had a broad smile. There was none like our "Cap," as we called him for short.

One day Cap was dividing his "catch" with us— two small red cabbages. We were so grateful; it was the only food we had. In fact, it was the only thing we'd had in the last couple of days. There was a knock on the door. When we opened it, and there stood a man, skinny as a beanpole, with his hat in his hand and tears in his eyes. Searching all our faces, his eyes settled on Cap.

The man begged, "Sir, do you have *any* food, anything at all? My wife is beside herself from hunger! I'm afraid she'll die!" Seeing the red cabbages, his eyes got as big as saucers.

Cap spontaneously gave him one of the cabbages.

"Sure, brother, it's not much, but it is all I have to give. Go with God and make sure, when you pray for your wife, to pray for others as well. Even your enemies." After the man left, Cap took a knife, cut the one remaining cabbage in half, and said, "The Lord has commanded us to live only a day at a time, and He will provide for tomorrow." That was faith! That captain exemplified the Christlike spirit. Indeed, he practiced what he preached.

The following day Cap learned from one of the countless people whose respect he had earned that there was a field where the cauliflower had been harvested the previous day. There were still some left to glean from the field. While Jake sat hidden in our attic room, Cap, Betty, and I walked the many miles to the field and back. We carried as many bags of the treasured vegetable as we could. We actually had to smuggle them back under cover of darkness. We were in danger of losing them to friend *or* foe. And if it was to the Nazis, we could lose our "privileges" such as ration cards, too. But though we did return safely with our "catch," we had no way of cooking the cauliflower. With his quick sense of humor, Cap said, "Anyway, if you chew it raw, it will last longer." We and many others ate cauliflower for breakfast, lunch, and dinner for the next several weeks—and survived!

On November 9, 1944, Jake could not take our dreary existence any longer. To be in constant hiding with never enough to eat drove him to distraction—and soon to *action.* One night he slipped away unexpectedly. In the morning, I found a note on the table, saying that he had left, on foot, long before dawn, to find food. He was determined to obtain it somehow, even if it meant trading some of my sheets and towels, which he had taken along. He was headed to the country to barter with the farmers. Because I did not know in which direction he had gone, I had no choice but to sit and wait. The danger of his being detected was certainly not imaginary, and it hung heavily on my mind. I foresaw disaster. The chance of our never seeing each other again was very real to me.

I felt there was no way out, but I knew from experience that ultimately the way was "up"; David the psalmist had said, "My help comes from the LORD, who made heaven and earth" (Psalm 121:2). That was my only source of peace. I was a bride of only two months and did not know where my husband had gone or if I would ever see him again! I could not know the danger he might be in, but I knew that, even in the darkest night, God had His eye on my Jake.

I waited all day in that upper attic room for the sound of his footsteps. I did not really expect his return in the daytime, so when evening fell, I listened even more closely, hoping more fervently that at any moment he would return. At seven o'clock the doorbell was pulled loudly. With a thumping heart, I opened the door and to my surprise, there stood Jake's lovely mother.

"Well," she said, "I just came home from a visit with one of the children when I found this note from Jake on the table. He must have come to my house and was worried for you."

> Dear Mother,
>   Please go and stay with Nettie tonight for I have gone for food. It will take me a few days and she will worry too much.
>   Love,
>   Jake

We embraced warmly. At first, utterly amazed, I did not say a word. It was three kilometers from her house to our apartment, yet she dared to come to me under the noses of the Nazis.

"Mother, they could have shot you! They don't allow us out after dark, you *know* that. They're on every street corner, and they're nervous about underground activities. So they shoot first and ask questions later!"

"Oh, child, I'm too clever for them, I fooled them by hiding in the shade of deep doorways, where my black clothing blended in so well. While they peered into the dark parts of the streets, I was near the streetlights, where they didn't expect anyone. I'd just wait until they marched off and then move quickly to my next hiding place. After all, I know this city so much better than *they* do. And that's how I got here safely!"

I hugged her again. "Mother, Mother, I love you for that. But you must be so hungry. I'm afraid that all I have is a little cauliflower."

"Hush, child! Hand me my purse." Her purse was legendary in our family. It might better have been called a valise. We used to joke about its contents, and she'd laugh like a child at our wild speculation. Now, as usual, it contained a rare treat: an apple, three big winter carrots, a little bottle of oil, and a special, even more unbelievable surprise.

"Mother, a bologna sandwich? I don't believe it! And all those other things; I haven't seen anything like that in ages! Where on earth did you get such a feast?" I somehow knew the answer myself: after a lifetime of giving to others, Jake's mother was being repaid. Those she had helped for years would never let her go hungry. Yet she knew how hungry I must be.

"Eat something, Nettie; that's why I smuggled all this under the Nazis' noses."

I stood up to get a knife and to wash the apple and the carrots.

"Don't peel them, child, even though you used to before the war. Remember that the best part is right under the skins."

"Oh, I won't, Mother. I'm just going to halve the apple and cut the ends from the carrots. And I think I'll add some cauliflower to make the whole dish more colorful."

We basked in the warmth of our reunion, Jake's mother and I. She asked then, "How is my son? He's my youngest, and I worry."

"He is so pale, Mother, so listless. When he's not sleeping, he's constantly talking about getting out of here. He's like a caged animal, and he's dreaming up crazy schemes. Last week we heard that the bridge one street over was being repaired with heavily tarred wooden blocks. Jake wanted to go over there with a pick hidden under his jacket and cut out some of those blocks for firewood. And he wanted to take along a burlap bag so he could carry more of those blocks. Even if he didn't get caught at the bridge, he'd stand out like a sore thumb with his full bag."

"You know how foolhardy that is; if they caught him, they'd shoot him on the spot. Why didn't you try to stop him, Nettie?"

"Oh, I can't influence him anymore. He's worried about the winter. It's so cold already, and it's only November. So he was determined. He wanted me to stay home, but I told him that if he was going to get shot, I'd get shot, too. At least, I thought he'd be more careful with me along."

Jake's mother nodded her approval. "Go on," she said.

"One night when it was overcast enough to limit the Germans' night vision, and raining hard enough to mask our footsteps, we made our move. I remember shuddering in the rain, but I knew it would also keep their patrols under cover. We had to be very careful in the poor visibility ourselves. You know there's no canal wall left since the bombing, so we could easily have walked straight into the canal. But we prayed. And we made our way by feeling for the edge of the sidewalk with our hands. We prayed again and made it safely across the highway and eventually to the railroad, which we knew would lead us to the bridge.

"We suddenly stopped; Jake's hand squeezed mine in warning. We heard voices. We almost stopped breathing, our hearts pounding. I expected a flashlight in my eyes, followed immediately by a shotgun blast in my belly. Instead, we heard the voices again, clearly now: 'I thought I heard something, Feite, but I guess not; is your bag as heavy as mine?'

"Mother, we knew then that they were like us. Jake suddenly said, 'Wait a minute, friends, please tell us where you found the wooden street.' Though they, like me, seemed startled by Jake's too-loud request, they showed us a place to start, right around the corner.

"There were many people there; I was so surprised. They worked hard while they could, in the rain; Jake, too. We filled our bags with the wet, tar-streaked pieces of wood that were as heavy as stones. Just as we were about to leave, Jake felt a small hand on his arm. An old woman begged, 'Please, I don't have any tools, would you loosen some blocks for me?'

"Well, Mother, you know how our Jake is. He

didn't rest until the old woman's purse was full of German firewood. But now I had a new worry: would we cross the bridge before daylight? Jake and I had just heaved our bags over our shoulders when someone yelled 'Hurry! hide!'

"Mother, I almost died of fright right there! The plaza was suddenly bathed in bright searchlights. Jake had dropped his bag, and I couldn't see him anywhere. German soldiers jumped out of their trucks and loaded them with the men and women they rounded up. I was safe; I had been under the bridge in shadow when the searchlight first blazed, but I didn't know about Jake. I thought they had him, and quickly I prayed for him. The lights went out and the trucks pulled away. And it was suddenly darker than before—in more ways than one.

"Suddenly, there was another miracle: Jake whispered my name. I cried, but he urged me to come quickly and go home with him. Mother, you have no idea what a close call that was! I wasn't that scared even by the bombing."

Jake's mother didn't say much. But I saw tears at the corner of her eyes, and I noticed that her lips were moving, though just barely. *Another private prayer?* I wondered to myself.

She was known by all of us as a woman of prayer. I never heard her pray aloud; although she did read her Bible for us, her praying was done in private, away from outside commotion. She had a face like an angel with beautiful white hair framing her pleasant, deeply wrinkled face. With her hands folded in reverence to our Almighty God, she was the strength of all the family.

She never stopped praying for her youngest son, Jake, who was the most likely to end up in Germany. One day during the early occupation, Jake

131

had been summoned to "enlist" in the German army. He had to go to a central point in Rotterdam to be examined by a doctor. Mother was upset about it and, to Jake's embarrassment, showed up in the room where a doctor was examining a row of men (including Jake), stripped to the waist. Every here and there stood a Nazi in full gear, keeping an eye on the doctors. The old doctor examining Jake motioned her over. He looked familiar somehow. He said, "Cato, is that you? Do you remember me?"

Mother exclaimed, "Oh, Barend, I thought I recognized you! How are you?" The doctor and mother had been friends in their youth, years ago.

Quickly looking to see how far away the Nazi overseer was, the doctor asked, "Is this your son?"

"Yes," Mother answered.

"Do you want him to go to Germany?"

Mother, who could cry at the snap of a finger, whispered, "No, of course not!"

Suddenly, he said, angrily, "Well, woman, why are you here? Get out of here, and go home."

At this commotion, the Nazi came to Mother and ordered her outside. The doctor and Jake followed, while the Nazi resumed his post. She thought: *What an animal that Barend is! First so nice and then so harsh.* Worry was written all over her face.

But the doctor said to Jake, with a wink: "You certainly have terrible rheumatism, don't you?"

Jake said, "Rheumatism? No, doctor, I don't."

"Then why am I giving you this official paper which disqualifies you for reasons of rheumatism?" He handed the paper to Jake with a smile, gently touched his mother's arm, and went back inside to resume his examinations.

The document Jake clutched in his hand meant freedom, at least for eight weeks, after which he'd have to be examined again. His "debilitating rheumatism" also entitled him to a few more food stamps.

In the midst of their relief, the thought came to Jake and his mother: What if the doctor had not known her?

In spite of myself, I too shuddered at the thought.

14

A Daring Plan

Early on the day after Jake's mother arrived at our apartment, there was a tumult outside. I went to inquire of our downstairs neighbors, who were quite upset. Before I could get the whole story the doorbell started ringing. When we opened it, there was the Gestapo in full gear with an announcement. It read: "On order of the Führer, all men between the ages of seventeen and forty are to stand in front of their homes immediately, dressed in warm clothes and strong shoes, with blankets, fork and spoon, and food for one day. Women and children are to remain in their houses. Anyone disobeying this order will be faced with the heaviest punishment to themselves and family. Anyone trying to escape will be shot."

After the Nazi left, Jake's mother started crying, "Oh, what will happen to Jake and his brothers?" We wondered whether the Nazis would only take those from a part of the city or from every neighborhood. We were especially afraid, because we lived on the Maas River and could see from our window the big flat ore boats waiting for the human "catch." More than fifty thousand men were stowed like cattle in those boats. All our homes were searched thoroughly. Had Jake been home, he would certainly have been found.

134

We wondered if Jake had been captured on his way home. There was no way to find out. We could not ask. Heavy machine guns kept wives and mothers from coming near the boats. The search for men and their loading onto the boats continued for two straight days. No one who lived there at that time will ever forget November 10th and 11th, 1944. When the boats finally left, a new stillness came over the entire city.

In that silence came two short knocks and a continued one on the outside door. It meant a friend, someone who understood our code. However, it was more than a friend, for when the door was opened, there stood my Jake. We both started crying and laughing at the same time. "Oh, Jake, oh, Jake," I cried, "Where have you been hiding? I thought they got you!"

"Tell us what happened," said Jake's mother while she helped him take his shoes off.

He said, "Mother, how nice that you're here; did you find my note?"

"Yes, but please tell us how you avoided getting caught."

Jake sighed and began; we hung on his every word: "When I neared home, a kind old man told me to beware of a big Nazi round up, a *razzia*. He said it was just in the back street, and he invited me to stay till the danger was over. When he later told me everything was safe, I rushed over here.

"And look what I was able to trade your sheets and tablecloth for to a farmer many miles from here: apples, potatoes, and a bag of oatmeal. I gave some also to the old man who warned me about the *razzia*."

I can never tell adequately how good our Lord is! What had seemed to me a disaster—my husband gone—became God's way of protecting Jake from being taken away on those ore boats. Jake's mother and I showered our love upon him. We continued talking about the miracle of those two days well into the night, holding hands in the darkness because no lights could be turned on. Many of our closest relatives had been captured, including two of Jake's brothers and a brother-in-law. Not knowing exactly why, Jake had been spared. I firmly believe it was part of the golden thread of God's care.

From that day, Jake had to hide not only from the Nazis, but also from any woman whose husband or son had been captured. These women became very bitter toward those who escaped. A price was set by the Gestapo for the capture or address of any man who did not report. Any mother with a hungry child would receive a loaf of bread if she was able to point out the hiding place of a fugitive. People were starving; the promise of a mere loaf of bread turned nice people in search of food into betrayers. Times were desperate. If one did not have a God to trust in, life was not worth the risk anymore.

Slowly the situation became worse. Cap had a hidden radio. Months before, we had been ordered to bring all radios to the central place, where they were soon in ruined heaps after the Nazis smashed them. Failure to obey this command had serious consequences. If one radio was found, everyone in that household could be shot. Some dared to disobey and hid them from view. We faithfully listened to "Radio Oranje," a station broadcasting from England solely to inform and encourage the suffering Dutch. Whatever news we heard, we spread by word of mouth. The radio had informed us about the Americans entering the war after Pearl Harbor. We learned about D-Day at Normandy, about Winston

Churchill and General Eisenhower. On many mornings we received further news from little cards with pictures of the royal family, Queen Wilhelmina exiled in England, and Princess Juliana with her children in Ottawa, Canada. These cards were dropped overnight from an English reconnaissance plane, much to the chagrin of the Nazis. On the opposite side of those cards were encouraging words that the war was almost ended. It kept our hope alive as the winter of 1944 approached.

But we became so weak, especially the men. Jake, a strong 165-pound, six-foot-tall young man, shrank to a slim 125 pounds. He looked so pale and skinny. He was neither sick nor healthy. He went through long periods of silence, too tired even to talk.

Information that Allied troops had taken over the southern part of Holland and all of Belgium gave us renewed hope. Night after night, as we heard the English planes on their way to bomb Germany, we knew that the war would end, and we would be free. As Christians, we tried to live even more closely to God. Cap preached one Sunday from 2 Chronicles 7:14:

> If . . . My people who are called by My name humble themselves and pray, and seek My face and turn from their wicked ways, then I will hear from heaven, will forgive their sin, and will heal their land.

Our prayer life deepened as we longed to live close to God. In such difficult times, when we are aware that any day can be our last, and if we believe in our all-knowing God, we will rely on Him for the smallest need. Daily I thanked God for a leader like Cap who helped us realize our priorities.

Even though we had had much to be encouraged by, the worst of the worst was still to come. We were

137

entering the winter described today in Dutch history books as the Hunger Winter. Only the strongest were able to survive this grueling ordeal. The women and children and older citizens made up the majority of the population. Even their rations had been cut to half a loaf of bread a week and one bowl of tulip-bulb soup per person each day. Many shared their small portions with hidden relatives. The plundering of our country had left it empty. There was no milk, no butter or oil, and no potatoes or other vegetables. Our only hope was that soon we would be freed.

Allied troops had taken over the southern part of the country. Freedom was so near. That was the good news. The bad news was that to end the war sooner, the Allied troops had decided to bypass Holland and drive straight to Germany. We were left to wait.

Both North Holland and South Holland are far below sea level and were protected by dykes. Many times when the bored Nazis had too much of their imported beer, they would drunkenly threaten to all who would listen, "Some day we will blow up those dykes, and all of you lowlanders will drown!" We thought it bluff, but that is exactly what happened in North Holland, where dykes were dynamited and all the land was flooded. So with the Allies bypassing us, the Nazis bragging about murdering us, and food scarce, death seemed imminent by one means or another.

In such times, people do strange things. It was no longer safe for anyone to know the whereabouts of any hidden person. Someone who could reveal the hiding place of a fugitive to the Nazis would be rewarded with a full loaf of bread. When your child is starving, who can judge? People in hiding could not stay at one address longer than one night. They used the rooftops to move from one house to the other. A woman could still move around in a city as big as ours, but men had to be hidden. It was even unsafe for their footsteps to be heard by neighbors. If we had not had our daily visit from Cap we could not have survived. He brought us the news from Radio Oranje and challenged us to keep our minds on the future when the war would be over. He also brought us something to eat, or at least to chew on. During that bitter cold winter, people stayed in bed, both to keep warm and to burn as little energy as possible. There were no closet doors, no closet shelves, no molding, no chairs anymore, because anything made of wood that wasn't essential had long since been burned for warmth. Even the wooden flooring in closets was used for heat. Forty-seven hundred people died that winter in the city of Rotterdam from hunger and cold alone.

One morning Jake woke up to discover that he was bleeding internally. We knew this was one of the early signs of death from hunger. We had to act fast. We had seen this happen to other people many times. Now it was happening to us. What should we do? In tears I went to Cap. He and Betty returned with me. After we knelt in prayer, Cap said, "I have a plan, but it is risky; however, so is staying here. You really have no choice. Outside on the building they are posting announcements. If any man comes out of hiding and voluntarily enlists to go to Germany his next of kin will receive a pound of lard and a full loaf of bread. Jake, do you have still the address of that Christian family in Nyverdal near the German border—the place where Nettie's sisters went after the bombardment of Rotterdam? Go and enlist. If they do not shoot you (for you cannot trust them) you may have a chance. You see, the Nazis are losing on every front, and the Americans are already on German soil. They need every man they can get, so you have a pretty good chance. They will put you on the train to Germany. When the train slows down after crossing the Ysel River, try to jump off to escape somehow and go to the Nyverdal address."

Jake agreed, but he was full of fear. I told him that I would wait a few weeks and then follow him on foot and somehow try to cross the Ysel River. The four of us knelt in prayer and commended Jake's well-being to the Lord. I went with him, shaking from the knowledge that this might be the last time we would be together. At the Gestapo station, Jake was immediately taken behind a wall and out of sight. Immediately, I expected the worst. Did they know about his phony rheumatism? Had they heard how he'd escaped the *razzia?* Or the roundup at the bridge, where we'd collected the "Nazi firewood"? At any moment, my worst fears might be echoed in the shots of a firing squad. I waited and waited until I saw him leave in an open army truck with a whole load of other skeleton-like men. In a way, I was relieved. But it was bitter cold, and his clothes were so thin.

Deeply troubled, clutching my loaf of bread and pound of lard—the trade for another human being—I made my way home. I climbed the stairs as though I had lead in my shoes. I felt so lonely, but Cap and Betty were there waiting for me. How urgently we prayed. How precious God is to His children. We were sure that somehow Jake would get to our friends in Nyverdal.

In the meantime, Jake was stowed with many other men like cattle in a box car. At least the

140

crowding kept them warm. The sound of the train's wheels on the tracks made the men sullen. They had no light, only the glimmer through the planks that made up the boxcar walls. No one spoke. Each man was alone with his own thoughts, hour after hour, farther and farther from home. Sometimes the train stopped, the door opened, and the light blinded their eyes. But they saw that only a few more men were thrown in, and as soon as the door closed the train would start again.

Suddenly, screeching brakes jarred them to a halt. The screaming and swearing of the Nazi guard made them all sit up. Doors were thrown open by soldiers with rifles. The men were ordered to line up; all the railway had been blown up by the Dutch underground. In all the confusion, Jake rolled into a ditch, crawled under the thick brush and waited it out. He said later that he thought the loud thumping of his heart would betray him. It seemed hours before the whole line of men marched off. Jake waited some more to make sure the guards wouldn't return and then walked to the nearest farm, where they told him he was near the German border, just twenty-five miles below Nyverdal. But *I* didn't know all that—not yet!

15

The Letter

Take the name of Jesus with you.
Child of sorrow and of woe;
It will joy and comfort give you,
Take it then where'er you go.

Precious name, Oh how sweet!
Hope of Earth and joy of Heaven

Take the name of Jesus ever
As a shield from every snare;
If temptations around you gather,
Breathe that Holy name in prayer.*

So many times before I had sung those words
when friends had to leave. Now the words echoed
through my mind. I had been debating for days
whether I should try to follow Jake. My heart did
not hesitate to say, "Yes!" But my common sense
made me realize that it was too difficult to try that
trip alone. And, I was scared. It was hard to make
up my mind. If I waited much longer, I knew I
would be too weak to make that long trip across the
country.

The ringing of the doorbell interrupted my
thoughts. I opened the door to see an old man
standing there with a letter in his hand. He showed

*Lydia Baxter, 1870.

142

me just enough to recognize Jake's handwriting, but he didn't give it to me. This stranger apparently made his living from situations like mine. He wanted food in exchange for that letter. I did not want to give this letter up, so I went to the almost-empty closet where only one item of food was left. It was the pound of Nazi lard received in exchange for my husband's freedom. I got a knife to cut a piece off for him, but he said that he wanted *all* of it in exchange for the letter. With tears of anger, I let it go. Taking that precious letter, I closed the door behind the parasite.

The letter was very short: "Arrived . . . come fast . . . I wait 10 days . . . will then return . . . Jake." I made up my mind; I would cross our country with the heavily guarded Ysel River in its center. I had talked to people who had come back unable to cross, but now I had to try anyway. Jake would return if I did not join him in ten days. It would mean death for him to come back.

I went to see Cap and Betty. She opened the door. Without small talk, I said, "Betty, I have a letter from Jake."

At that Cap came out of the kitchen and said, "That's unbelievable; no one gets mail any more!"

"How did you get it?" Betty asked.

Cap was impatient: "Let me see the letter." He read it aloud and then said, "Thank God he is safe; I hope he doesn't get it in his head to come back."

I agreed, "That's why I'm here. I want to go after him!"

Betty was aghast, "Alone? Are you out of your mind? Remember Vrouw Bakker? She tried such a walk sometime back and is still too sick even to come out into the street! Jake is safe where he is, and you are safe here. It is irresponsible to go all alone!"

Cap disagreed, "That's all well and good, but you know that sooner or later, Jake will come back for Nettie!"

I was glad Cap understood. "I will take my time; if I leave early tomorrow morning, I should be able to make it in five or six days."

Cap's sensible solution was predictable. "Why don't we pray? If God did not want Nettie to go, this letter would have never been delivered. Mind ye," he added more to himself than to anyone else, "that letter is a miracle in itself. It traveled from hand to hand across a distance of two hundred kilometers in less than a week."

And so we knelt, the three of us. Cap spoke as a son speaks to his Father. He presented all our concerns (and there were many) to the One who had been and would continue to be my Strength, my Fortress, and my Protector. It was true I had lost a lot of weight, but I had lost none of my determination. I knew that my Lord would be with me all the way.

After a restless night, I packed a small alarm clock, a few pieces of clothing, a toothbrush, one loaf of bread, and a small Bible into a shoulder bag and went to say good-bye. Cap, Betty, and a few older friends who were in on the plans gave me my final instructions. They were very concerned for my safety. Cap took me aside and, with big wrinkles in his usually happy face, confessed his biggest worry. "Nettie, I did not sleep much last night. You are a young woman about to travel through unknown territory. There are hundreds of troops around, men away from their sweethearts. Some have not seen their loved ones for months or even years. You are in grave danger. We cannot be of much more help, other than to commit you into the hand of God. But remember, you like to sing and you know many songs by heart. My advice to you is this: when you sense danger or when you have to pass soldiers on the road, don't look left or right, but fasten your eyes to the point ahead and sing as loudly as you can. Sing any hymn that comes to your mind. When they hear you, they will either join in with you or think you're crazy. Either way, you will have a better chance of having them leave you alone. The Lord will be your companion.

"As soon as you enter a city," he continued, "search for Christians. Ask for a Salvation Army Corps, look for a church." He handed me a letter of recommendation. Then we knelt to pray and sing, ending with the words, "Take the name of Jesus with you!"

We said good-bye. I hesitated and turned. "I wish you could go with me."

"Well," he said, "we thought about it, but a captain never leaves his ship."

Such loving, faithful servants of the heavenly Father—would I ever see them again? I looked back only once as I rounded the corner, but then I was alone.

I had to cross the Northern Island, so I stopped to see if my mother had returned from Goudriaan. She had gone to visit the farmer family where my youngest sister Kobie had found refuge after the bombing of Rotterdam. These people had been very good to Mother, supplying her with extra food—much of what they themselves had been able to keep from the Germans—to supplement her rations from the central kitchen. How glad I was that she opened the door when I rang the bell. I sat down to explain my situation to her.

Mother sat across from me at the kitchen table.

"Where are you going, Nettie?" she asked with a questioning look at my small pack.

"Mother, when you were away, Jake came down with the same sickness that so many people have before they die of hunger. So we agreed that his only chance was to volunteer to be sent to Germany, hoping to escape after crossing the Ysel River. I never thought that I would hear from him again, but I did."

Producing the scribbled letter, I said, "A miracle happened. Look here; he is safe and sound in Nyverdal. Now I am going there, too."

I expected her to argue, but she didn't. "That's a good idea. I still get enough food for myself from the family with which your sister lived, but that will not be enough for both of us."

Satisfied that her needs for the coming months were supplied, I felt better in leaving her. She waved to me until we could not see each other anymore. Now I was really on my way.

I had lost much time, so I hurried along until I came to a highway. It seemed an endless ribbon of road in front of me. Here and there I passed other people walking, mostly in small groups. My first goal was the beautiful city of Utrecht, known for its waterways and its central cathedral. It was a fifty-five kilometer walk, and I expected it to take at least two days. I was far from being in good condition, tiring easily. I saved time by not stopping to eat. I had only one loaf of bread and just took a bite when I could not keep my stomach from growling.

Doubts were troubling my mind. I thought I might as well make this a hymn-singing journey. Of course, not every song is a marching song, but on that day, many a slow psalm instantly became a rhythmic melody. I had been obliged to learn many

146

hymns by heart, because like many others, I had not had a personal songbook. It had been customary in our services to repeat a song until everyone knew it from memory. The first one I began singing was

> Rock of ages, cleft for me,
> Let me hide myself in thee;*

The words of another came to mind.

> Take my life and let it be
> Consecrated, Lord, to Thee;
> Take my hands and let them move
> At the impulse of Thy love,
> At the impulse of Thy love.†

I kept singing old favorite songs and choruses. I didn't care that people looked at me and thought me a bit strange. I had to be in the right frame of mind if I was to survive the ordeal ahead. And singing helped.

I had already walked for more than an hour on this road, and all kinds of vehicles—from horse-drawn carts to trucks and bicycles—were passing me by. Many were filled with people fortunate enough to get a ride either by paying for it or by sheer luck. Suddenly, I heard my name called. It came from the horse-drawn wagon that had just passed. The wagon stopped, and off jumped two smiling young women, daughters of a woman that Mother knew from her church. There were on their way to relatives in Soest, a small village just past Utrecht. They invited me to ride with them. I realized that even there, the golden thread of God's care was being woven. It was a wonder that they recognized me among all the travelers. I told them how

---

*Augustus M. Toplady, 1776.
†Frances R. Havergal, 1874.

they were the answer to the prayers offered just that morning. They shortened my two day journey to just a few hours.

Arriving at the city of Utrecht, I was dropped off at the Red Cross center where the refugees from Amsterdam, Rotterdam, and Utrecht congregated. Many people passed through Utrecht, all obsessed with escaping certain death from hunger. They all were to try to cross the Ysel River. We had been told that *there was food* across the river and that many farmers there were willing to share it. But at that center were people with the defeat written on their faces. They had tried to cross and were on their way back. One women tried desperately to persuade me to give up. "I was there for days" she said, "I slept there, pleading with the guards at the bridge; nothing helped. It is a long way back from there, don't go; return to Rotterdam with me." I assured her that my method of crossing would be better than hers. In the meantime, volunteers at the Red Cross center provided me with a warm fluid that seemed a cross between coffee, tea, and mud; but it *was* warm. I got a cot to sleep on.

The next morning, I awoke early and started on my way alone, leaving the tumult of the Red Cross center behind me. I thought I would have a much better chance of being offered a ride while traveling by myself—indeed, if there was any ride to be offered! The close fellowship between my Lord and me helped me face the challenges which lay before me. Hunger was my biggest enemy. I was reluctant to eat from the loaf of bread in my shoulder bag, but soon I could resist no longer. I nibbled a big corner from the loaf, for I felt a huge hole in the center of my body where my stomach was located. To escape thinking too much about that particular problem, I started singing again:

There shall be showers of blessing:
This is the promise of love;
There shall be seasons refreshing,
Sent from the Savior above.*

I thought of the many times I had heard Jake play this melody on his trombone. I was doubly determined to get to Jake as fast as I could. Still singing, I turned a corner and found myself smack in the midst of a troop of laughing, mocking Nazis. They were guarding a small bridge over the canal that I had to cross. There were so many of them! Looking up, I instantly reacted to the advice Cap had given me. I began to sing all the louder. All of a sudden I stopped in my tracks and stopped my singing, because the nearby air raid siren went off.

Instantly the whole scene changed. All the blustering, mocking Nazis ran like frightened rabbits to an air raid shelter nearby. I too looked around for shelter. A woman came riding by on a bicycle. She was terrified. Throwing her bicycle aside, she grabbed my neck and screamed, "Oh, I am so afraid! I am so glad to see another woman."

A small English plane dove over that bridge and dropped a bomb on it. Immediately the Germans retaliated with machine gun fire. The little plane had made a turn and was coming back. I looked around and saw a manhole made for emergencies like this. I yelled to the woman to jump first. She did, and I was all ready to jump after her when she screamed. The pit was full of quicksand. I knew that if quicksand gets a good hold on you, you just sink deeper until it buries you. I pulled the bicycle over the hole so she could get a good grip on it, and she pulled herself out, all covered with that light yellow

*Daniel W. Whittle, 1883.

gooey quicksand. Strange as it seems, we screamed with laughter, while all around us the bombing of the bridge continued. There is a proverb that says, "Laughter does good like a medicine" (cf. Proverbs 17:22).

It was apparent to me that those Nazis would be angry, looking for revenge at any minute. I knew I did not want to be around when they came out of their air raid shelters, but how would I get to the other side of the canal? The frightened woman had now pulled herself together and I was able to tell her about my situation. She was from that very neighborhood and knew the area well.

"Where are you going, anyway?"

"Over the Ysel River. But how do I get away fast enough over this waterway?"

"Hurry, climb on the back of my bike; I'll *row* you over at our place." Peddling hard, she got us away from our oppressors. She showed me where we could safely cross the canal behind her house. I thanked her, and thanked God *for* her. I thanked Him that I was not attacked and that I could again be on my way.

This trip was teaching me a step-by-step reliance on my Lord. The golden thread of His care was evident wherever I turned. That evening I reached Amersfoord.

Again, I did not worry about a place to sleep. The Red Cross had a post at the crossroad. They gave me a cot and something warm to drink. The Red Cross volunteers treated and bandaged the big blisters on my feet. The bandages filled in the spaces left by the holes that had worn through my socks. I had started out with two pairs of heavy socks, but only one pair of already well-worn shoes. The soles were thin, but I had hoped they would last until the war was over. I was also concerned about my bread supply. I had been so hungry that I had eaten too much. There was only one third of the loaf left, and the hole in my stomach seemed bigger than ever!

I believed tomorrow would be better. As I sat down on my cot, I took the little Bible out of my shoulder bag. I read a very familiar and comforting passage from John 14:1-3:

> Let not your heart be troubled; believe in God, believe also in Me. In My Father's house are many dwelling places; if it were not so, I would have told you; I go to prepare a place for you . . . I will come again, and receive you to Myself; that where I am, there you may be also.

As I continued reading that chapter, I came across the words of Jesus in verse 27:

> Peace, I leave with you; My peace I give to you; not as the world gives, do I give to you. Let not your heart be troubled, nor let it be fearful.

I read until my eyes got heavy under the very dim light, and I fell asleep peacefully.

16

Crossing the Ysel

Always an early riser, I awoke before anyone else. I had a long walk in front of me. It would probably take me two more full days—Amersfoord—Apeldoorn. I did not have to wait for breakfast. It was now each one for himself. I could not stand the hunger much longer. I still had a little bit of my bread left. I nibbled more than I had planned, and this stopped (at least temporarily) the painful gnawing in my stomach. Several times I thought I should just give up. Often I did not know what to do, but one thing I had learned fast was to trust my heavenly Father completely for everything. I knew He was aware of my dire needs. In the past, I had been well provided for and so it would be this day.

I had only to put my shoes on, and I would be on my way. No matter how I tried, I could not force my swollen feet into my shoes. There was no other way but to cut the toes out and make them into sandals.

There were two ways to cross over the Ysel River. One way led over the highway to the bridge in Deventer. The safer way was the southern route over Zutfen, but it was twenty-five miles longer. Not only that, but I would not be walking alone. Many others were there, also wanting to cross the Ysel. They would probably take the advice of the Red Cross volunteers and travel the much longer but safer southern route. I had been too tired the night before to listen to all the pros and cons of taking a road so much farther south. They tried to change my mind, but I was afraid Jake would leave for Rotterdam if he did not see me soon. I knew that could mean certain death for him.

After leaving that morning, I traveled on what was called the "Carcass Highway." It got its name because every two miles or so lay the bullet-riddled carcass of a bombed truck. There was not a single person or anything else as far as my eyes could see. It was frightening, to say the least. The best medicine for me to get my mind off my troubles was to start singing again.

> What can wash away my sin?
> Nothing but the blood of Jesus;
> What can make me whole again?
> Nothing but the blood of Jesus.
>
> O! precious is the flow
> That makes me white as snow;
> No other fount I know,
> Nothing but the blood of Jesus.*

I loved singing. It helped me to forget my big problem temporarily. I went from songs to choruses to psalms and whatever I could set to a familiar tune. Sometimes I murdered the tempo of a slow song just to accommodate my walking. I walked that forsaken road for several hours, never seeing a moving truck, nor a bicycle, nor a living soul. My feet were so sore that I had to sit down, but it was too cold, and I had to keep moving. I had eaten my last bit of bread in the afternoon. The little alarm clock I carried showed that it was only 2:30. I could

---

*Robert Lowry, 1876.

not set one foot in front of the other any longer.

For the last few miles, tears had been rolling down my face. Fear overcame me with questions that seemed to have no answers. "Did God forget about me? Did He not care anymore? Had it all been just an illusion? Was it all just in my mind? Was I going to die here?" I sat down under one of the trees by the side of the road and took my shoes and socks off. My feet were bleeding. Today's blisters had formed on top of yesterday's; shoes with too-thin soles had caused my feet to swell and bleed. I was so discouraged, so hungry! I asked God to please let me die. I must have fallen off to sleep from pure exhaustion, with my shoulder bag at my side.

The sound of a truck woke me. I could see it coming in the distance. But I could not stand on my feet to get the driver's attention. I prayed "Lord, hear me; please let the driver stop, or else I'll die here." About a hundred feet away there was a carcass from another truck strewn all over the road. That truck maneuvered with great skill and unbelievable speed around the scattered debris. I prayed all the more earnestly, "Oh, Lord, let him stop, please let him stop."

Are you ever surprised when God answers your prayer so instantly? I should not have been! Does it not say in His Word, "God is our refuge and our strength, a very present help in trouble"? Had not my whole life been interwoven with the golden thread of His care? This all flashed through my mind in a split second. I saw the truck sway from left to right and come to a halt against the branches of the tree where I was sitting. Out jumped a man in his mid-forties, swearing and cursing because he had a flat tire. He got out and took a look at his truck, then stopped abruptly when he saw me. Walking slowly toward me, he said, "What in the world are you doing here on this dangerous road?" He talked as though he were my father. "Lucky for you," he continued, "that I had a flat tire."

"I prayed that you would stop, somehow," I answered. His eyebrows went up in surprise, and he sat down next to me. As he talked to me, he opened a neatly wrapped liverwurst sandwich.

"Are you hungry, too?" When I nodded, he went to his cab and got one for me, too. I never tasted anything that good! Not only was I starved, but I had not even smelled meat for I don't know how long. I ate the sandwich slowly, turning it around and around in my mouth while answering his questions. I explained that I was on my way to Nyverdal to meet my husband and that I planned to go over Apeldoorn to Deventer to cross the Ysel River.

"Impossible," the man said. "That bridge is so fortified with troops, you'll never make it. You have to go to Zutfen. There are only four guards there most of the time. They usually do not inspect me, for I go that way frequently and they know me. You can ride on my truck. First I have to repair my tire, though. You take your time to eat and get your shoes on."

That was easier said than done. My feet were bleeding and swollen. I left my socks off; even so, I could barely get into my shoes. When I stood up, I nearly fainted. Taking them off again, I tied the laces together and hung the shoes around my neck. I wore only my socks. It was impossible to do otherwise. I was shivering from the cold and the misery when the man came to tell me he was ready.

He gave careful instructions that were to be followed to the letter: "This road is under constant surveillance by the English to prevent any transportation out of the area. If they find us, we will be bombed or strafed out of existence. I cannot be responsible for you in any way after I start driving. It will be a grueling experience for you, but if you make it, you will be over the Ysel River by nightfall. I have no room in my cab, but I can tie you on top of the wood and you can hold onto the outside of the cab. I will be driving at high speed, for I have driven this section many times. It is dangerous. We'll cross over the bridge in Zutfen, if we can. Most times they just wave me through, but many times they also stop me. If they do, they will search through everything. If you are discovered, I will pretend that I did not know you were there. You will have to find your own way of crossing the bridge. I have to deliver this cargo farther south."

Then he said something which brought even greater fear: "Watch the skies, and keep your ears open. If a British plane is coming, I will stop suddenly, and abandon the truck. You'd better follow me to safety as fast as you can. The truck will be destroyed immediately. You'll have to run for your life." Looking at me, he said, "I am sorry. That is the only chance you have."

I said, "Then we'd better pray." Seeing that the man was willing to do so, I prayed for protection for him and me. "You'd better keep praying the whole trip," he said.

I had not looked at the back of the truck. When I saw where I was to ride, I almost died of fear. The load of wood he carried was cut up and stacked to its fullest, peaking high in the back of the truck. On that stack of wiggling wood I had to "hang on" the rest of the way to the Zutfen bridge. The man tied me to the cab and gave me part of the rope. He said, "Pull that rope if you have to get off; then slide down as fast as you can and start running." There was just one handle on the cab to hold onto. When we were finally on our way, I thought the truck was being driven by a maniac. Not only did he drive fast, but to avoid hitting the debris in the road, he swerved left and right. I held on and kept a close watch on the sky.

I was so preoccupied with fear that I never prayed. I was just plain scared stiff for my life. I've learned since that people back home were bathing me with prayer. How good to belong to the family of God! When I could not pray, they did!

When the bridge came into view, I was very much aware that there was no place for me to hide. Strangely though, the guards didn't order me off the truck. But we had to wait. Soon, a Nazi inspection crew took over and demanded that I get off but paid no further attention to me. I found myself in the midst of hundreds of people who were all just as determined to cross the wide Ysel River in front of us. Homes all around were in ruins. I feared that, if I could not get to the other side, I would die here. I could not walk back, but neither could I walk forward. I began to question the pitiful group in front of the bridge. "How long have you been here? Do you know anyone who's made it across? Is there really food on the other side?" What a hopeless looking bunch! Some had been there for almost a week, not knowing where to go or what to do. There was no food, and nobody seemed to care. Their reactions were sullen—most of them merely looked up without answering or just shrugged their shoulders when I asked about our chance of crossing.

I couldn't stay with such gloomy people. I remembered Cap's advice: Look for Christians. I began to move out of the crowd and away from the bridge. Almost unable to move my battered, swollen feet, I prayed for wisdom. There were a few houses still standing, and I noticed children playing marbles in front of one of them. I approached them and asked if they knew whether there was a Salvation Army in their town. One of the girls looked up at me and announced, "We belong to the Salvation Army. Would you like to speak to my parents?"

I was dumbfounded and said, "Oh, please, would you mind?" The girl picked up my bag and helped me to her house, just a short distance away. I went through my pitifully meager belongings to find the letter of recommendation Cap had given me. I handed it to the girl's parents and was immediately welcomed into their home. The family was just beginning to gather at the table for a real Dutch meal—"hutspot," a casserole of carrots, onion, and potatoes. They invited me to share their meal. I had not had a warm meal in many months. I did not mention this to them, but accepted their most gracious invitation. I could not stop my tears as the blessing was asked. I was again in awe of the golden thread of God's care.

After the meal was over, the whole family— mother, father, and their three children—gathered in the living room. They apparently had something to talk over. "Well," the father said to the children, "Get ready, there's a job to do." To my amazement, they got their hats and coats and brought out a typical Dutch leather shopping bag, the kind the women take with them to the market. They placed my shoulder bag in it, and clothed me in an old black raincoat. They gave me a babushka for my head and a pair of slippers for my sore feet. Then that father (whose name I was never to know) explained the plan to me.

"In just a little more than ten minutes the watch over the bridge will be changed. Wait until a truck comes to be inspected. Two of the four Nazis will inspect that truckload, and only two men will be left to hold back that whole mass of people. It will keep them very busy. Then, with my two children about you, pretend to be their mother. They will yell hello to the guards; they have made special "friends" with them just for this purpose. Do not look up or down, but walk straight to the other side of the bridge. The children will return a couple of hours later when the watch has changed again and the new guards cannot know that they had someone with them when they crossed earlier. We have friends on the other side where they will stay until the danger is over. Go with God, and you will never be alone. We will pray that all goes well." And with that he brought us to the door.

I wanted to ask, "What about the danger you bring to your own family, and what about your children?" But the door was closed quickly and the children hurried me along. I realized then that I did not even know their names. What a mission these people had!

There was no time to lose. "Hurry," the children whispered. As we approached the bridge, there still was a large crowd of people standing about, but the two girls, probably eleven and nine years of age, pulled me along without saying a word. Very quickly, just as the father had said, a big double trailer truck came to the bridge. The driver was stopped for inspection by the two guards. While the two other guards took over, these two young children pulled me ahead and said not to walk too fast. I heard the guard shout for us to stop and expected then and there to get a bullet in the back. But the children kept walking and called back, "Hi, Fritz! Hi, Heinrich!" Ignoring the call of the guard to return, they kept on going. I walked with dread, praying all the way.

Halfway across the huge bridge, the children turned to me and said, "We are safe now; there are no guards on the other side." I could not believe it yet. On the other side, larger areas lay in ruins. But in the midst of it all, several homes still stood. Near one of them I sat down and just cried my heart out. The two little girls dried my tears as if I really were their mother. They asked, "May we have our mother's coat and babushka now?" Placing these two items in the leather shopping bag and giving me back my shoulder bag, they ran away. I called to them, but they yelled back that they had strict orders just to drop me off on the other side, and that was all.

Some people came out of one of the unharmed houses and told me that in a whole week not one person had passed over that bridge. I knew that I served a great God, but every time He showed His power anew, I stood amazed, as I still do today. These people took me into their home, with no questions asked. One brought a tub of warm water and Vaseline. They washed and bandaged my feet. After I had a good night's sleep in a soft bed, they prepared breakfast for me, which included an egg. What wonderful medicine—rest *and* an egg! A lifetime of service to my Savior and Lord cannot portray the love I owe Him for seeing me through in such a miraculous way. Had I remained back in Amersfoord with a *group* of women, I probably would not have survived.

These new "nameless people" (all underground people were nameless for safety reasons) invited me to stay for a few days. I would have loved to, but I was so afraid that Jake would leave for Rotterdam. So with a bag full of sandwiches and a lot of advice, I set out for Nyverdal. My feet were packed in two pairs of hand-knitted socks. The slippers were exchanged for a pair of shoes, only they were a size too big. They felt so much better though, and my stomach no longer growled, for I had eaten more food in the past day than I would have had in Rotterdam for several weeks. I started to sing again:

> My Jesus, I love Thee,
> I know Thou art mine;
> For Thee all the follies
> of sin I resign;
> My gracious Redeemer,
> my Savior art Thou;
> If ever I loved Thee,
> My Jesus, 'tis now.*

I continued with

> What a Friend we have in Jesus,
> All our sins and griefs to bear!
> What a privilege to carry
> Everything to God in prayer!
> O what peace we often forfeit,
> O what needless pain we bear,
> All because we do not carry
> Everything to God in prayer!†

I stopped only for short periods, but I started to tire sooner than I had on the previous day. I ceased my singing to concentrate on a point in the distance, and then I tried to reach it and to set a new goal. Finally I gave up and knocked on a farmhouse door. There were dogs barking as a man came to the

*William R. Featherstone, c1862.
†Joseph M. Scriven, 1855.

door. I politely explained to him my desire to reach my husband and asked if I might sleep in the barn. Looking at his face, I expected that he would send me away, but his wife said before he could say a word, "William, let her sleep in the hay loft."

"It will be OK." The man reluctantly gave his permission. I supposed that he had once had a bad experience letting someone sleep in the barn. Thousands upon thousands had fled in the past five years, and it was quite likely that I was not the first to knock on their door.

The wife was very understanding. She took a lantern with her and showed me the way to the barn. She sat down to talk a bit. "So you came from Rotterdam? Well, have you heard the good news then?" I shook my head. "General Eisenhower is negotiating for the three locked-in cities. The Nazis are furious with the continued losses and have threatened to break the dykes as they did in the North and South of the country. If they do this, it will cost thousands more lives. So the world is watching, wondering what will come of their threat. The Americans have heard the plea of our people. They have sent many planes and are dropping loads of food in the open fields at the outskirts of Rotterdam."

I could not believe my ears. I was beside myself with joy, though I knew that for many of my family, neighbors, and friends, help would be almost too late. The woman added, "Any day now, the American troops will be here, and we will all be free!" Then she said goodnight and left.

I was too excited to sleep. Could it really be true that the war would end soon? I could no longer imagine what it would be like. I prayed for the Americans to get here soon and added, "Lord, thank You, thank You for giving me this good news!"

And maybe tomorrow I would meet my Jake in Nyverdal! My elation was tempered, though, by doubts. What if Jake had already left to find me in Rotterdam? After all, the ten days he talked about in his note were almost over. And he was a man of his word. "No, he couldn't!" I despaired. "I can't make the trip back anymore!"

I resorted again to prayer, a source which would never run dry for me. "Keep him safe, Lord. Don't let him be captured. Please . . ."

In my exhaustion, my heavenly Father quickly put me to sleep and spared me dreams.

17

Nyverdal

At that very moment, Jake was pacing back and forth on a farm near Nyverdal, waiting for word about his wife. Each day made him more impatient. Feeling guilty, he kept thinking, "I should never have left Nettie alone. What if she stayed in Rotterdam, with nothing to eat? She could die, and here I am not able to help her." Other times as he paced to and fro, he would wonder, "What if she is on her way—all those miles—alone?" At last he sat down with his head in his hands and cried out, "Oh, God, be merciful—watch over her—bring her to me, please!"

There was very little Jake could do to pass the time. After his arrival in Nyverdal the Tolson family had kindly found a farmer who could use him for little jobs. In return, Jake received food. Other than that, he just waited. Those Dutch farmers helped not only Jake but thousands of refugees who sought hiding places in their remote farmhouses and barns.

Radio Oranje provided frequent news of the advancing American and Canadian forces. Night after night, the sky was full of the droning of planes on their way from England to bomb Germany. Each night the Nazi searchlights scanned the skies for English planes entering or returning from Germany. If they were successful in shooting down a plane, they would also try to shoot the parachuting pilot. The Nazi soldiers would drive their vehicles as fast as possible over the fields. But our men were also watching, in shifts. As soon as the pilot's feet touched the ground, one would take him away, while another would wait to cover the whole scene up with hay; by the time the Nazis searched everywhere, the pilot would be watching from atop a hay loft, sometimes coming very close to being found.

It was funny to watch the Nazis searching furiously for a man already safely hidden just a few feet away. But some men were captured in spite of the efforts to conceal them.

The farmers, their neighbors' farms in clear view, developed a unique way of alerting each other to danger. Every day a few pieces of laundry were kept on the clothes line. This in itself meant nothing. It only helped conceal the presence of one lone white sheet waving in the wind. The single sheet meant all was well. If Nazi soldiers arrived at any farm, the wife went out and hung more wash and a second sheet. The second sheet meant "Beware!" If a third sheet was hung out, it meant that the Nazis were there and alerted everyone without passport to go into hiding. These heroic farmers hid the escaped pilots and refugees, along with hundreds of escaped Jewish children, in an underground family of refugees. At night they could all hear the war far off in the distance. The news from underground sources was most encouraging; it gave the refugees hope that their long days of hiding would soon end.

The farm work helped to pass the time, but many rainy days had delayed the sowing season. The days just dragged by for the men in hiding. The only thing that Jake found worthwhile was to keep his eye on the road to Nyverdal, for that lay to the

165

southwest, the direction from which the Allies would arrive. *Soon,* hoped Jake.

One day Jake told the farmer, "If my wife has not come by tomorrow night, I will go back to her." Against the advice of all his new family members, he prepared to return to Rotterdam. It would be a monumental task, one which he might not survive. But he had already waited longer than he intended to. First he would have to cross the heather fields. When in full bloom, these beautiful fields were purple. Now they were filled with hard brown stubby bushes pushing out of the sandy soil. It would make hard going, but it was the safest way, and Jake was determined.

The following morning, after saying good-bye to the farmer, Jake was nearing the first outlying houses when three young girls came running toward him. They were the Tolson children, the new friends he had made. He began to walk faster toward them, because they appeared to have news.

Waving their arms they shouted, "Your wife is here! Your wife is here!" Jake started running and never stopped until he arrived in the living room of our friends and found himself in my arms. We didn't know whether to laugh or to cry. But he soon started to fuss about my bleeding feet. The last part of my trip over the heather fields had really taken its toll on them.

At that moment, I wasn't concerned about my feet or anything else, for I was so happy to be with Jake. I wanted to know everything that had happened to him. I kept staring at him. Even though he was still awfully thin, his color was changed from a grayish white to tan, an outward sign of improvement. "They tried to fatten me up with warm cooked cereal, bouillon, and light tea at first," he said, "but now I eat regular food, and my stomach does not hurt any more. Yet I am constantly hungry, even a half-hour after I eat supper." While I was talking with Jake, the Tolsons brought me a glass of warm milk and a soft-boiled egg, and so it was all the time. Everyone tried to outdo each other in caring for me.

In the midst of our happy reunion came one shadow: we would not be able to stay together at the same place. There was no room for both of us, because three families already lived in that one home. So Jake reluctantly returned to his own farmer. A place near Almelo, close to the German border, was arranged for me. We were to be about eight miles from one another. We didn't complain about this arrangement, though, because we were confident that the war would soon be over. Then we could return together to Rotterdam. How we could ever have survived without the help of all those good-hearted people is beyond all imagination! Everyone made the best of a bad situation. And many came to know Christ as their personal Savior in those difficult times.

Jake prayed constantly for my care, as I did for him. How much we needed those prayers, for in the next ten days our entire area became no-man's land, a strip of land between two fighting armies—a living hell! It all started while I was sleeping that first night. The advancing American army, which had conquered France, Belgium, and part of the Netherlands, was now within ten miles of us. Hitler's troops were retreating. General Eisenhower, in charge of the Allied troops, commanded the English to bomb every bridge or road that led into Germany. I found myself right in the path of that fleeing German army and I was unable to escape the incessant bombing. This past five years, I had been through many bombings. Whether it was the unfamiliar territory or the loneliness I felt without Jake, I do not recall, but I was frightened beyond words—more than ever before. In my mind, these were the worst ten days of the war for me.

With haste, the people I now lived with pulled me along with the others into an empty grain silo already prepared with enough food and blankets to last for a while. But the tops of the silos were partly open. We could hear the screaming of children frightened by the heavy firing both from the advancing Allies and the retreating Germans. Our prayer became urgent, "Lord, end it soon!" The fear of being trapped in that place or even buried alive was very real. As soon as there was the slightest break in the firing, someone would peek through our one trap door and shout, "American." This would cause our hearts to rejoice. Another time a head would appear through the door and shout, "German." This would make us tremble with fear.

For ten days, our area was either in the hands of Americans or Nazis. And we could not move in either case. If anyone in that silo had never prayed before, he or she quickly learned that it was the only hope of survival. One day, almost two weeks later, the air was silent for several hours, and we began to breathe easier. Suddenly, we heard church bells ringing in the distance. What could it mean?

Someone yelled, "We are free!" The news was passed to the others in the silo. Free? Could it be true? We could hardly believe our ears, but people started coming toward our silo from all directions. We dared to come out of the silo, where people were hysterical, laughing and crying. Right in front of us stood an American tank, and out came the most

handsome, smiling soldier that any of us had ever seen. More good-looking soldiers came out of that tank; they were so tall and looked so well fed!

We went absolutely crazy. People climbed on top of the tank. We draped the tank in Dutch flags, which had been unused for the past five years. Our tears were tears of jubilation, because those years of slavery had just ended in joy. We hugged the Americans and called them "Yankees," a name we felt expressed our love. They waved and smiled and threw bubble gum to the kids and cigarettes to the adults.

All of a sudden we saw from afar a German truck coming at high speed. Instinctively, fear welled up in us, but the Americans didn't seem to notice. When they drew nearer, we saw why: the huge Swastika had been covered over with four words, "Long Live the Queen." On top were men in dark blue coveralls. They had broad smiling faces, and their helmets were nonchalantly tilted. Everyone but me seemed to know who they were. I asked a jubilant woman: "Who are they?"

Proud as she could be, she answered, "Those are *our* men! Our secret Dutch underground army. All local men. They are heroes. They blew up the railroad and the bridges. They stormed the S. S. headquarters and destroyed all the important files. That woman over there lost her husband in one of those raids." She pointed to a woman embracing a boy and a girl. "And do you see that old man crying? He lost his only son. Yes, these men in the underground are very brave."

One of the men in that truck, seemingly the leader, stood up to shout, "Long live the queen!" Then after waving the crowd into silence, he spoke. "People, finally the war is won, and you are all to come to the marketplace for the celebration." As the crowd renewed their cheers, the Dutch patriots again started their truck; waving, they headed off to other farms to spread the news.

I walked to the marketplace with the talkative woman. She said, "Did you see that tall young man on the truck? That was my son. His father is somewhere in Germany—captured."

I looked at her suddenly sad face. "Yes, but that's soon over. Your son is back now and your husband soon will be, now that the war is over."

"Yes," she said with new hope.

I did not dare spoil her dream by telling her of my own deep worry. Where was Jake? Where in the world could I find him? Would he be lost or even. . . ? "No, No! Oh, Lord, let me find him!"

Suddenly, I again heard the woman, "I am talking to you; is there something wrong?" Then and there, on the long country road, passing the loud-singing people on the way to the marketplace, I cried. Between sobs I managed to blurt out, "I do not know where my husband Jake is, nor where we would ever find each other. I've come so far!" I cried some more and sobbed out my whole story.

She said, "Don't worry, everyone will come to the marketplace in Almelo—every villager, every farmer. I am sure you'll find him there."

To make me think about something else, she exclaimed, "Oh, look at the home of van Vliet; it is almost completely demolished, but still, there's our beautiful flag blowing in the wind! Oh, and there's Maggie!" And before I knew it, they were hugging and kissing while four children romped around them. They were certainly not the typical Dutch straw-haired children; they had beautiful black shiny eyes in small white faces. They were Jewish children hidden for these years, unnoticed by family or neighbors. Maggie and her husband Gerrit were two unsung heroes. Sheltering these Jewish children could have cost them hard labor or even death in a concentration camp.

The jubilant crowd on the country road swelled in numbers. Many children were dressed in orange, for our beloved Queen Wilhelmina was of the House of Orange.

All of a sudden the door of a house near the road opened and out came two fully-uniformed English pilots, blinking in the bright sunlight. They had been hidden for months from the frantically searching enemies. Now they could not move, for they were surrounded by the jubilant Dutch, who insisted that they lead the parade to the marketplace. When that throng then met a tank full of American soldiers, there was no end to the joy.

In the marketplace, I looked frantically for Jake, but it seemed futile. Suddenly, in the midst of my despair, I felt a hand on my arm; turning, I saw that it was my Jake. Neither of us felt it strange or unusual that we were crying in each other's arms.

Epilogue

From the distance came a familiar sound. We could not see through the crowd, but as the sound came nearer, we knew that it was the Salvation Army band. We managed to find a spot where we could push through the masses, and there we saw the flags—the familiar red, white, and blue-striped flag of the Netherlands, and next to it the Blood and Fire Christian banner of the Salvation Army—the two symbols of our nation and our God, side by side. The band stopped in the center of the marketplace. The men removed their caps, and the mothers hushed their children. Then all in one voice we sang one of the old songs of faith.

> Now thank we all our God
> With hearts and hands and voices,
> Who wondrous things hath done,
> In whom His world rejoices;
> Who from our mothers' arms,
> Hath blessed us on our way
> With countless gifts of love,
> And still is ours today.

All praise and thanks to God
The Father now be given,
The Son, and Him who reigns
With them in highest heaven,
The one eternal God,
Whom earth and heaven adore;
For thus it was, is now,
And shall be evermore.*

Freely we cried, man and woman alike. The unbelievable had happened; we had survived. Even though 200,000 Dutch had lost their lives, and 100,000 Dutch Jews were murdered in concentration camps, we had made it through the most grueling of wars.

Jake and I stood with our arms around each other, like two dots in the universe, so poor but so rich. We were sure in knowledge that the Almighty God, maker of heaven and earth, would lead our next steps.

The golden thread of His love, His care for us His children, would remain forever unbroken.

---

*Martin Rinkart, 1636, trans. Catherine Winkworth, 1858.